T0389632

Secularisation in Australian Education since 1910

Religion and Education

Editor-in-Chief

Stephen G. Parker (*University of Worcester*)

Associate Editors

Jenny Berglund (*Stockholm University*)
Leslie J. Francis (*University of Warwick*)
David Lewin (*University of Strathclyde*)
Deirdre Raftery (*University College Dublin*)

Volumes published in this Brill Research Perspectives title are listed at *brill.com/rpres*

Secularisation in Australian Education since 1910

By

Clarissa Carden

BRILL

LEIDEN | BOSTON

Library of Congress Control Number: 2021915924

Typeface for the Latin, Greek, and Cyrillic scripts: "Brill". See and download: brill.com/brill-typeface.

ISSN 2772-2597
ISBN 978-90-04-50347-2 (paperback)
ISBN 978-90-04-50348-9 (e-book)

Copyright 2021 by Clarissa Carden. Published by Koninklijke Brill NV, Leiden, The Netherlands.
Koninklijke Brill NV incorporates the imprints Brill, Brill Nijhoff, Brill Hotei, Brill Schöningh, Brill Fink, Brill mentis, Vandenhoeck & Ruprecht, Böhlau Verlag and V&R Unipress.
Koninklijke Brill NV reserves the right to protect this publication against unauthorized use. Requests for re-use and/or translations must be addressed to Koninklijke Brill NV via brill.com or copyright.com.

This book is printed on acid-free paper and produced in a sustainable manner.

Contents

List of Tables   VI

Abstract   1

Keywords   1

Part 1: Secularisation and Australian Education: Definitions
and Approaches   1

  Introduction   1

  Secularisation: The Approach Used in This Book   4

  The Plan of This Book   14

Part 2: Religious Instruction and State Schools: Expansion and Constraint in
the Early Twentieth Century   15

  Introduction   15

  "Free, Secular, and Compulsory" Education in Australian History   16

  *Case Study 1: Shared Christianity and the Introduction of Religious
  Instruction to Queensland State Schools*   19

  Case Study 2: German Schools and the Limits of Shared Christianity   29

  Conclusion   39

Part 3: Government and Non-government Schools: Questions of Faith,
Choice, and Control in the 1960s and 1970s   40

  Introduction   40

  Public Funding and Christian Schools   41

  Social Science and Humanities Education and the Christian Right   45

  Case Study 3: The Introduction of Federal Funding for Religious Schools   46

  *Case Study 4: Banning MACOS and SEMP: A Local Victory for the
  Religious Right*   57

  Conclusion   68

Part 4: Twenty-First Century Debates: Christian Influence
in a Complex System   69

  Introduction   69

  Secular Systems? Religion in Contemporary Australian Education   69

  Case Study 5: Challenges to School Chaplaincy   72

  Case Study 6: Simultaneous Fights in Queensland   81

  Conclusion   95

Part 5: Conclusion   95

Acknowledgements   97

Tables

1 Key movements in secularisation theory 4
2 Dimensions of secularisation 8
3 Key moments in the history of the Bible in State Schools League 21
4 Major events in the closure of German schools 30
5 Key moments in the introduction of state aid for private schools 48
6 Key moments in the banning of MACOS and SEMP 58
7 Major events in Australian school chaplaincy, 2011–2015 73
8 Key moments in the introduction of Safe Schools and the review of religious instruction materials 84

Secularisation in Australian Education since 1910

Clarissa Carden
Griffith University, Brisbane, Australia
clarissa.carden@griffith.edu.au

Abstract

This book aims to provide an account of the complex nature of secularisation in the context of Australian primary and secondary education. Drawing on the sociological literature on secularisation alongside historical, sociological, and broader interdisciplinary scholarship on the relationship between Christian and secular belief systems in Australian education, it seeks to complicate understandings of what it means to have a secular education system. Each part examines a different period in Australian schooling, providing both a synthesis of key literature and an examination of original case studies.

Keywords

secularisation – Australian education – Australian schooling – religious education – religious instruction – controversies in education – conflict in education

Part 1: Secularisation and Australian Education: Definitions and Approaches

Introduction

The 'secular principle' is well-established as a trait of Australian governance and public education. Yet the extent to which any system of education in Australia can be described as 'secular,' and indeed what this term means, is unsettled. Remy Low has identified three key trends in the historiography of the 'secular' in Australian schooling, stating that:

> While the various associative interpretations of the history of Australian schooling emphasise different aspects of how the secular came to be one of its defining features, they tend to agree on three points: that the secular principle in schooling was accomplished by the putting aside of differences for agreement – whether of common citizenship or procedural

© CLARISSA CARDEN, 2021 | DOI:10.1163/9789004503489_002

fairness; that this secured an education that was and is neutral amidst differences; and as such, the secular principle abets social fairness, inclusion and cohesion in the nation.[1]

Low argues that "the political arrangements that define schooling as secular are not the outcome of inevitable laws of progress or ideal principles, but a result of contingent and contested turns in the political history of colonial invasion in Australia."[2] These "contingent and contested turns" have contributed to shifting definitions of the term 'secular.' The centrality of the 'secular' concept to perceptions of Australian schooling also raises questions about how, in what circumstances, and with what consequences, the 'secular principle' is contested.

This work builds on my 2018 Ph.D. thesis, where I drew on Foucault's "history of the present"[3] to uncover the complex and contingent development of the relationship of what I describe as 'Christian' and 'secular' impulses specifically in the education system of the Australian state of Queensland.[4] In this work, I position the case studies examined in my dissertation in conversation with the broader literature on 'Christian' and 'secular' settlements in Australia. Through a combination of fine-grained historical case studies and sociological theory, this monograph aims to contribute to bridging the gap between the approaches of historians and sociologists in understanding the relationship between dominant faith groups and 'secular' ideals in educational contexts.

While some sociologists have produced valuable studies of the extent to which Australian schools may be considered secular, their work has, almost by necessity, taken a broad approach.[5] Local particularities are obscured in favour of presenting an account of the national situation. Yet historical, or historically-influenced, scholarship focused on specific case studies has revealed the distinct nature of what might be described as 'secular settlements' in the

---

1   Remy Low, 'Secularism, Race, Religion and the Public Instruction Act of 1880 in NSW', *History of Education Review* 48, no. 2 (26 September 2019): 175, https://doi.org/10.1108/HER-07-2018-0019.

2   Ibid., 176.

3   Michel Foucault, *Discipline and Punish: The Birth of the Prison*, trans. Alan Sheridan, 2nd ed. (New York: Vintage Books, 1995).

4   Clarissa Carden, 'Turning Points: Christian and Secular Battlelines in the History and Present of Queensland Education' (Doctor of Philosophy, Brisbane, Australia, Griffith University, 2018).

5   E.g. Cathy Byrne, *Religion in Secular Education: What, in Heaven's Name, Are We Teaching Our Children?*, International Studies in Religion and Society 21 (Leiden Boston: Brill, 2014); Marion Maddox, *Taking God to School: The End of Australia's Egalitarian Education?* (Sydney: Allen & Unwin, 2014).

varying Australian states and territories.[6] At times, these works have argued for a more careful examination of the complexities of 'secularisation' and of what it means for a schooling system to be 'secular.'[7] Yet, as Stephen Jackson identifies, this body of historical research has largely focused on the nineteenth century, when such settlements were initially laid down, at the expense of other, equally significant, moments.[8] This has limited examinations of how settlements have changed and developed, and of what "secular" education means today.

In this context, this monograph has two key aims. Firstly, it seeks to provide a more complex account of the relationship between Christian and secular impulses in Australian education than is possible within a study of a single case. It accomplishes this through an examination of the scholarship on this relationship alongside six distinct case studies. Each part focuses on a period of conflict and change and seeks to identify the diverse forces at play in defining and redefining what it means to advocate for 'Christian' or 'secular' positions in education. Secondly, the book aims to argue for the continued utility of secularisation as a theoretical perspective in understanding changes in the relationship between religion and education. In support of this aim, this chapter synthesises the sociological literature on secularisation, developing a definition which, I argue, offers a useful way to conceptualise the 'battlelines' drawn between proponents of different belief systems at key historical moments and to understand how and why 'secular settlements' have been refined, revised, and rewritten.

6　Clarissa Carden, 'Bibles in State Schools: Moral Formation in the Late Nineteenth and Early Twentieth Century Queensland School', *History of Education Review* 47, no. 1 (4 June 2018): 16–24, https://doi.org/10.1108/HER-07-2016-0029; Stephen Chavura, "'… but in Its Proper Place…." Religion, Enlightenment, and Australia's Secular Heritage: The Case of Robert Lowe in Colonial NSW 1842–1850: Robert Lowe and the Secular in NSW', *Journal of Religious History* 38, no. 3 (September 2014): 356–76, https://doi.org/10.1111/1467-9809.12075; Stephen James Jackson, "'Not in the Business of Indoctrination": Religious Education in South Australian Public Schools, 1968–1980', *History of Education Review* 49, no. 2 (16 October 2020): 249–62, https://doi.org/10.1108/HER-01-2020-0006; Low, 'Secularism, Race, Religion and the Public Instruction Act of 1880 in NSW'; Remy Low, 'A Genealogy of the Secular versus Religious Schooling Debate in New South Wales (Part 1): Terror and Suspicion', *Journal of Religious Education* 62, no. 1 (April 2014): 25–38, https://doi.org/10.1007/s40839-014-0003-4; Remy Low, 'A Genealogy of the Religious versus Secular Schooling Debate in New South Wales (Part 2): Populism and Patriotism', *Journal of Religious Education* 62, no. 2 (July 2014): 53–64, https://doi.org/10.1007/s40839-014-0006-1.

7　Carden, 'Turning Points'; Carden, 'Bibles in State Schools'; Chavura, "'… but in Its Proper Place…." Religion, Enlightenment, and Australia's Secular Heritage'; Jackson, "'Not in the Business of Indoctrination".

8　Jackson, "'Not in the Business of Indoctrination", 250.

The case studies selected in this work all relate, to an extent, to the system of schooling in Queensland, Australia. While some focus on issues of national significance, the use of cases from a single state is instructive in providing evidence of how the national landscape described in the literature is reflected, or not reflected, within more local contexts.

Secularisation: The Approach Used in This Book

Defining secularisation is complex due to the vast body of existing, often contradictory, literature. In Table 1, I identify some of the key movements in the development of secularisation theory. Naturally, this is only a partial account. As this table demonstrates, even among scholars who agree that 'secularisation' is a useful theoretical tool, there are significant differences of opinion as to what the term entails and how secularisation ought to be measured. Identifying a useful definition is further problematized by confusion about the social changes which may be defined as occurring within the context of secularisation, and by a tendency to conflate secularisation with religious change or to assume that secularisation, and the very idea of the 'secular,' are

TABLE 1   Key movements in secularisation theory

Movement	Perspective	Illustrative scholars
Classical theory of secularisation	Secularisation is occurring. The changes associated with modernity (the establishment of science as a truth and knowledge system which shapes how people live, judge and relate to the cosmos) will necessitate a decline in religious authority and participation.	Weber,[a] Durkheim[b]
1960s and 1970s secularisation theory	Secularisation is occurring and is defined by the differentiation of church and state. This was a movement characterised by a	Berger,[c] Fenn,[d] Wilson[e]

a   Max Weber, *The Protestant Ethic and the Spirit of Capitalism*, Routledge Classics (London; New York: Routledge, 2001).
b   Émile Durkheim, *The Division of Labor in Society* (London: Free Press, 1964).
c   Peter L Berger, *The Sacred Canopy: Elements of a Sociological Theory of Religion* (Garden City, New York: Anchor Books, 1969).
d   Richard K Fenn, *Toward a Theory of Secularization*, Monograph Series – Society for the Scientific Study of Religion, No. 1 (Storrs, Conn.: Society for the Scientific Study of Religion, 1978).
e   Bryan R Wilson, *Religion in Secular Society: A Sociological Comment* (London: C.A. Watts & Co Ltd, 1966); Bryan R Wilson, *Contemporary Transformations of Religion* (Oxford: Clarendon Press, 1979); Bryan R Wilson, *Religion in Secular Society: Fifty Years On* (Oxford: Oxford University Press, 2016).

SECULARISATION IN AUSTRALIAN EDUCATION SINCE 1910

TABLE 1   Key movements in secularisation theory (*cont.*)

Movement	Perspective	Illustrative scholars
	significant level of sociological interest in secularisation. It produced several idiosyncratic approaches to the phenomenon. Secularisation theorists at this time agreed that the decline of religious authority was at the heart of the secularisation process.	
Neo-secularisation	Secularisation is occurring at multiple levels. Focused not on the decline of individual religiosity but the decline of religious authority. Some of the most important work in this movement seeks to systemise the theories produced during the 1960s and 1970s. This movement sees scholars seeking to address the critiques of a growing body of work arguing that the theory of secularisation is false.	Tschannen,[f] Chaves,[g] Dobbelaere[h]
Post-secularism/late secularism	Secularisation has occurred, but there is no evidence that religion will necessarily continue to decline or disappear in the face of modernity. Social changes such as immigration, involvement in conflicts based on religious principles, and the increasing presence of religion in public debate have changed public consciousness about religion. Christianity has declined but religiosity (incorporating people from multiple faith traditions) remains strong. Late secularism suggests that despite the	Habermas,[i] Possamai[j]

---

f   Olivier Tschannen, 'The Secularization Paradigm: A Systematization', *Journal for the Scientific Study of Religion* 30, no. 4 (1991): 395–415.

g   Mark Chaves, 'Secularization as Declining Religious Authority', *Social Forces* 72, no. 3 (1994): 749–74.

h   Karel Dobbelaere, *Secularization: An Analysis at Three Levels*, 2. print, Gods, Humans and Religions 1 (Bruxelles: PIE Lang, 2004).

i   Jürgen Habermas, 'Notes on Post-Secular Society', *New Perspectives Quarterly* 25, no. 4 (2008): 17–29.

j   Adam Possamai, 'Post-Secularism in Multiple Modernities', *Journal of Sociology* 53, no. 4 (2017): 822–35.

TABLE 1 Key movements in secularisation theory (*cont.*)

Movement	Perspective	Illustrative scholars
	many types of relationships between religion and secularism, it is still correct to say that we are living in a secular age. Compatible with the theory of multiple modernities. This movement engages with criticism of the theory of secularisation.	
Late secularisation	Secularisation has occurred and, in Western nations, continues to occur. Engages with critiques that hold that secularisation has not occurred or has ceased to occur. Recognises that declines in practice do not necessarily respond to equivalent declines in belief. There are diverse and conflicting perspectives within the movement, especially in relation to determining when a decline in Christian significance began.	Bruce,[k] Brown,[l] McLeod[m]

k Steve Bruce, 'The Sociology of Late Secularization: Social Divisions and Religiosity: The Sociology of Late Secularization', *The British Journal of Sociology* 67, no. 4 (December 2016): 613–31, https://doi.org/10.1111/1468-4446.12219.

l Callum G Brown, *The Death of Christian Britain: Understanding Secularisation, 1800–2000*, 2nd ed., Christianity and Society in the Modern World (London; New York: Routledge, 2009).

m Hugh McLeod, 'The Crisis of Christianity in the West: Etering a Post-Christian Era?', in *The Cambridge History of Christianity*, ed. Hugh McLeod, 1st ed. (Cambridge University Press, 2006), 323–47, https://doi.org/10.1017/CHOL9780521815000.019.

inherently opposed to the continued existence of religion.[9] Perhaps the greatest problem of all is the presumption that modernity and secularisation are necessarily linked, and that the narrative of secularisation in modernity is a linear one.

9 As critiqued by both opponents to secularisation theory and proponents of a more nuanced, revised, perspective. Rodney Stark, 'Secularization, R.I.P.', *Sociology of Religion* 60, no. 3 (1999): 249–73; Rodney Stark, 'Secularization: The Myth of Religious Decline', *Fides et Historia; Terre Haute* 30, no. 2 (Summer 1998): 1; Mark Chaves, 'Secularization as Declining Religious Authority', *Social Forces* 72, no. 3 (1994): 749–74; Chavura, '"… but in Its Proper Place…." Religion, Enlightenment, and Australia's Secular Heritage'.

While no definition will satisfy all theorists, secularisation has the potential to enhance explanations of the role of religious groups, particularly dominant groups, within national or state-based education systems. To do so, however, it must be responsive to what Jackson describes as the "gradations of secularity" which may exist within schooling systems.[10] That is, it must not assume that there has been a simple, linear transition from a religious society to a secular one, nor should it presume that secularisation occurs in the same way in all local contexts, even within a single nation.

In this text, I define secularisation as a social phenomenon that is historically and culturally specific, changing and recursive, which is situated in existing power relations, and which is multi-scalar and multi-dimensional. The definition I propose does not presume that secularisation occurs alongside modernisation, or indeed that there is only one way to be modern, and is, instead, compatible with what Eisenstadt has described as "multiple modernities."[11] Table 2 provides an overview of the definition used in this book and the most significant scholarship used in its development.

This revised definition is, I will demonstrate, useful due to its ability to explain instances of decline and expansion in Christian dominance over schooling systems in a way that does not rely on the presumption of ongoing decline. It is further useful insofar as it opens up the possibility of interrogating shifts in the meaning of secular and Christian ideologies, rather than presuming that such ideologies hold consistent meanings over time. In doing so, it recognises that, as Chavura et al. argue in a recent work, "the concept of the secular receives its full meaning from the cultural context in which the word is used."[12]

Component 1: Secularisation Is Historically, Culturally, and Spatially Specific

The first key dimension of secularisation is that it historically, culturally and spatially specific. This is an argument proffered by Casanova, who states that, while the secularisation of Europe "is an undeniable social fact," this secularisation is, in fact, confined to Europe itself and to some former European colonies.[13] For him, secularisation is a culturally specific phenomenon, which has become accepted as a necessary part of modernisation, due to the influence

---

10   Jackson, "'Not in the Business of Indoctrination'".

11   Shmuel Noah Eisenstadt, 'Multiple Modernities', *Daedalus* 129, no. 1 (2000): 1–29.

12   Stephen A Chavura, John Gascoigne, and Ian Tregenza, *Reason, Religion, and the Australian Polity*, 2020, 9.

13   José Casanova, 'Cosmopolitanism, the Clash of Civilizations and Multiple Modernities', ed. Reimon Bachika and Markus S Schulz, *Current Sociology* 59, no. 2 (March 2011): 255, https://doi.org/10.1177/0011392110391162.

TABLE 2   Dimensions of secularisation

Dimension	Description	Key theorists
1. Historically, culturally, and spatially specific	Both religion and secularisation are specific to the society and historical moment in which they are studied. Even very similar societies may have different experiences.	**Neo-secularisation:** Casanova[a] **Post-secularism/late secularism:** Martin[b]
2. Changing and recursive	Secularisation is not linear. Periods of desecularisation or religious revival may occur.	**1960s and 1970s secularisation:** Wilson[c] **Neo-secularisation:** Dobbelaere,[d] Tschannen[e]
3. Situated in power relations	Neither religion nor secularisation can be understood separately from the broader structures of power in which they are situated.	**1960s and 1970s secularisation:** Berger,[f] Wilson[g]
4. Multi-faceted and multi-scalar	Secularisation is geographically situated. It occurs or does not occur in specific places. Further, it can be analysed at different levels. These levels support the analysis of changes including	**Neo-secularisation:** Dobbelaere[h] **Post-secularism/late secularism:** Possamai,[i] Wilford[j]

a   José Casanova, 'Cosmopolitanism, the Clash of Civilizations and Multiple Modernities', ed. Reimon Bachika and Markus S Schulz, *Current Sociology* 59, no. 2 (March 2011): 252–67, https://doi.org/10.1177/0011392110391162.

b   David Martin, 'Secularization: An International Debate from a British Perspective', *Society* 51, no. 5 (October 2014): 464–71, https://doi.org/10.1007/s12115-014-9812-z.

c   Wilson, *Contemporary Transformations of Religion.*

d   Dobbelaere, *Secularization.*

e   Tschannen, 'The Secularization Paradigm: A Systematization'.

f   Berger, *The Sacred Canopy*; Peter L. Berger, *The Social Reality of Religion* (Middlesex, England: Penguin University Books, 1973).

g   Wilson, *Religion in Secular Society: A Sociological Comment.*

h   Dobbelaere, *Secularization.*

i   Adam Possamai, *Religion and Popular Culture: A Hyper-Real Testament*, Gods, Humans, and Religions, no. 7 (New York: P.I.E.-Peter Lang, 2005).

j   Justin Wilford, 'Sacred Archipelagos: Geographies of Secularization', *Progress in Human Geography* 34, no. 3 (June 2010): 328–48, https://doi.org/10.1177/0309132509348558.

SECULARISATION IN AUSTRALIAN EDUCATION SINCE 1910   9

TABLE 2   Dimensions of secularisation (*cont.*)

Dimension	Description	Key theorists
	but not limited to the societal differentiation between church and state and the reduction of individual belief.	
5. Can be understood in relation to multiple modernities	Just as there is more than one way to be modern, there is more than one way for a modern society to relate to religion.	**Post secularism/late secularism:** Possamai,[k] Martin[l]

k   Possamai, 'Post-Secularism in Multiple Modernities'.
l   David Martin, 'Secularisation and the Future of Christianity', *Journal of Contemporary Religion* 20, no. 2 (May 2005): 145–60, https://doi.org/10.1080/13537900500067687; Martin, 'Secularization'.

of predominantly European sociologists. Even the most vigorous proponents of the secularisation theory have noted that a very different pattern of secularisation occurs in Europe, where there has often been a state church, compared to the United States, which was founded on the assumption of religious, or at least denominational, pluralism.[14]

Similarly, David Martin argues that it is possible to look at differences in cultural contexts which may not be, on their face, related to religion, and find that they are nonetheless related to how secularisation as an ideal, and a set of processes, operates within these contexts.[15] Martin's analysis reveals that secularisation is not the result of a single change, but of many, often contradictory, changes. He argues that a historical analysis of secularisation should recognise these changes, which may be modest, without obscuring the reality that they are specific to the circumstances in which they occur, and that countermovements are possible.

Component 2: Secularisation Is Changing and Recursive

The second, related, component of secularisation as it is used in this book is that it is shifting, changing, and recursive. This is in line with the thinking of

14   Bryan R Wilson, *Religion in Secular Society: A Sociological Comment* (London: C.A. Watts & Co Ltd, 1966), 101.
15   David Martin, 'Secularization: An International Debate from a British Perspective', *Society* 51, no. 5 (October 2014): 464–71, https://doi.org/10.1007/s12115-014-9812-z.

neo-secularisation theorists such as Dobbelaere and Tschannen, both of whom argue that secularisation is not linear.[16] Instead, they indicate, it is dependent upon historical processes which are sensitive to cultural change and which may be reversed. For Dobbelaere in particular, secularisation is far from an ongoing progressive force. Instead, it is accompanied by processes of desecularisation and resecularisation, through which churches may regain lost authority and social influence or, alternatively, lose the power they have regained. While I identify this component as emerging broadly from the neo-secularisation movement of the 1990s and 2000s, the possibility of religious revitalisation was recognised even during the 1960s and 1970s movement. For example, Wilson suggested that, even in the context of a secularised or secularising society, specific pockets of religious belief can experience revival or growth.[17] For Wilson, though, desecularisation was expected to occur within specific places and communities, not necessarily on a broader cultural level.

Component 3: Secularisation Is Embedded in Existing Power Relations

A third aspect of defining secularisation is that it is embedded in power relations. This has been recognised in the work of the 1960s and 1970s with, for instance, Berger arguing that religion provides an important justification for social institutions.[18] A useful theory of secularisation must also recognise that churches can retain power and authority recognized even by those who do not hold religious beliefs. For example, Wilson notes that churches can play an important part in offering "appropriate ceremonial for prestige and status-enhancement at crucial stages of the life-cycle," particularly for events like baptisms, weddings, and funerals.[19] This ceremonial prestige is particularly significant in relation to the public mourning of official war histories and events of serious social upheaval.

Component 4: Secularisation Is Multi-faceted and Multi-scalar

In keeping with a recognition of the relevance of the specificities of cultural and political context, the definition of secularisation employed in this book is

---

16   Karel Dobbelaere, *Secularization: An Analysis at Three Levels*, 2. print, Gods, Humans and Religions 1 (Bruxelles: PIE Lang, 2004); Olivier Tschannen, 'The Secularization Paradigm: A Systematization', *Journal for the Scientific Study of Religion* 30, no. 4 (1991): 395–415.

17   Bryan R Wilson, *Contemporary Transformations of Religion* (Oxford: Clarendon Press, 1979), 37.

18   Peter L Berger, *The Social Reality of Religion* (Middlesex, England: Penguin University Books, 1973), 42.

19   Wilson, *Religion in Secular Society: A Sociological Comment*, 18.

multi-scalar and multi-dimensional. By this, I mean that it recognises, not only large-scale transformations of society, and not only the mass decline of individual religiosity, but also the subtler shifts and changes through which secularisation, or its opposite, what may be described as desecularisation, may occur.

Dobbelaere takes up this argument, proposing that secularisation takes place at three levels: societal secularisation, organisational secularisation, and individual secularisation.[20] In recognising that secularisation can occur at these levels, he also suggests that it is possible for desecularisation, understood as a reversal of the secularisation process, to occur at the same levels. Understanding these different spaces and processes of secularisation allows the sociologist to uncover the interrelations between the three. Dividing the analysis between these three levels also helps to overcome the tendency to differentiate between the 'public' and 'private' sphere, with the latter viewed as a space in which religion may be present, but which cannot be analysed as part of public forms of secularisation.[21] While Dobbelaere's analysis provides an important tool in demonstrating the scales and dimensions along which secularisation may take place, it also has the potential to obscure the subtleties of secularisation processes. It is important to take this analysis as suggestive, not conclusive.

Dobbelaere's concept of "societal secularisation" refers to a process through which the values of organised religion become increasingly irrelevant for the legitimation of everyday life. This is the result of processes of differentiation – the quintessential separation of church and state. It can occur through deliberate policy or latently, as an unintended consequence of actions intended to promote rationality or differentiation of sub-systems in society. Talcott Parsons highlights the significance of denominations in causing this separation to occur.[22] Societal secularisation may occur, for example, through the differentiation of education from religion or politics. It can also result in attempts by religious groups to counter the reduction of religious influence in such differentiated spaces.[23]

"Organisational secularisation," another concept emerging from Dobbelaere's synthesis, occurs within a religion. This requires that religions become more worldly, more concerned with everyday life rather than with transcendental meaning. Churches undergoing this process may adopt the values of the

---

20   Dobbelaere, *Secularization*.
21   Ibid., 103.
22   Talcott Parsons, *Structure and Process in Modern Societies* (New York: The Free Press, 1981), 295.
23   Dobbelaere, *Secularization*, 19–20.

secular society in which they are positioned. This can enable churches to leverage their value and influence through providing services and forms of care that the state neglects or seeks to hand over to non-government organisations. The adoption of values associated with a broader secular society may occur through an active declaration of secular values or a subtler shift to a more open and less negative relationship with popular ideals and cultures. They may alternatively undergo a reversal of this process and seek to re-sacralise religious life.[24] This is a phenomenon that is evident, for example, at Christmas and Easter, where churches often seek to open a conversation about the religious meaning of these holidays.

For Dobbelaere, "individual secularisation" is associated with a decrease in individual commitment to, and integration in, religious bodies.[25] Examining individual secularisation implies uncovering the closeness – or otherwise – of the beliefs and practices of individual actors to those prescribed by religious groups, including those to which the individuals may subscribe.[26] Despite the limitations of this type of categorisation, the recognition of multiple levels inherent in Dobbelaere's analysis helps to understand tensions like that noted by Possamai, who states that while it appears to be the case that "traditional institutional religion' is declining, there are nonetheless still people who experience religion and religious experiences in their everyday life, and people who believe in God or something similar."[27] Using Dobbelaere's terminology, it can be suggested that this observation reflects a situation in which societal secularisation has occurred, but individual belief remains potent. Similarly, McLeod has argued that the weakening of Christian belief in the West has not necessarily kept pace with the decline in practice.[28]

The idea that secularisation is multi-scalar has been taken up by geographers, including Wilford, who argues that a multi-scalar and multi-faceted understanding of secularisation offers much to the analysis of the relationship between religion and place.[29] For Wilford, it is necessary to recognise the possibility of religious entrepreneurs filling "archipelagos:" particular spaces in

---

24   Ibid., 22.

25   Ibid., 137.

26   Ibid., 25.

27   Adam Possamai, *Religion and Popular Culture: A Hyper-Real Testament*, Gods, Humans, and Religions, no. 7 (New York: P.I.E.-Peter Lang, 2005), 32.

28   Hugh McLeod, 'The Crisis of Christianity in the West: Etering a Post-Christian Era?', in *The Cambridge History of Christianity*, ed. Hugh McLeod, 1st ed. (Cambridge University Press, 2006), 325, https://doi.org/10.1017/CHOL9780521815000.019.

29   Justin Wilford, 'Sacred Archipelagos: Geographies of Secularization', *Progress in Human Geography* 34, no. 3 (June 2010): 328–48, https://doi.org/10.1177/0309132509348558.

which it is possible to sacralise everyday life.[30] Similarly, Gao et al. show that, even in the context of a secular or secularising nation-state, specific groups such as migrant workers can reinvigorate the sacred in the locations in which they live.[31] While this work focuses on the resacralisation of local spaces, other research explores the public sphere with Possamai arguing that a "re-invasion of religion in the public sphere" has occurred.[32] A useful definition of secularisation would recognise that the secularisation is spatialized and that revivals in the public sphere or in local "archipelagos," exist alongside other, fragmented and potentially very different, changes in the relationships between religious and secular ideals.

Component 5: Secularisation Can Be Understood in Relation to Multiple Modernities

A final factor in a useful definition of secularisation is that it must take into account the existence of what Eisenstadt has called "multiple modernities."[33] This term refers to the reality that modernisation has not occurred evenly or followed the same path throughout the world. There are, for Eisenstadt, multiple modernities because there are many pathways to modernity and many ways to be modern. Given the historical intimacy between the ideas of secularisation and modernisation, the recognition of multiple modernities helps to illuminate the cultural specificity of secularisation. The recognition of multiple modernities helps to explain the limitation in some sociological accounts of secularisation highlighted by David Martin, who states that "even when sociologists deal with the past they are selective, because only approved routes to modernity, like ascetic Protestantism, are allowed to count."[34] In this sense, Martin contributes to the argument that sociologists are themselves both products and authors of the complexity of modernity and that, in managing this complexity, they can reduce perspectives to those that are manageable and coherent. In essence, his argument indicates that the perspectives sociologists choose frame ways of seeing and not seeing, which obscure or remove from the representational frame cases which offer contradictions or challenges to established theory. They ignore the varying local forms of secularisation, which may

---

30   Ibid., 343.
31   Quan Gao, Junxi Qian, and Zhenjie Yuan, 'Multi-Scaled Secularization or Postsecular Present? Christianity and Migrant Workers in Shenzhen, China', *Cultural Geographies*, 2018, 1474474018762814.
32   Possamai, *Religion and Popular Culture*, 33.
33   Eisenstadt, 'Multiple Modernities'.
34   David Martin, 'Secularisation and the Future of Christianity', *Journal of Contemporary Religion* 20, no. 2 (May 2005): 145, https://doi.org/10.1080/13537900500067687.

occur in a manner different from that anticipated by the master narrative, just as they ignore the resurgence of particular forms of religious identities. For Martin, alternative master narratives focusing on particular belief systems rather than, or in addition to, secularism can help sociologists to think about multiple modernities as they relate to religiosity. Martin reiterates the importance of cultural context in understanding secularisation, stating that:

> When we study secularization from a comparative cultural perspective we do not simply compare figures of belief and practice. We look at how people in different societies are embedded in structures of power and webs of culture, and how they place themselves in the narratives of history, especially the narratives of national history as constructed by local elites.[35]

From this perspective, the utility of secularisation as a theoretical frame is dependent upon the ability of the researcher to understand the studied culture in terms of power relations, histories, and ways of knowing.

The idea of multiple modernities is also taken up by Possamai and Spohn, respectively,[36] who view it as enabling a more mindful approach to the geographical and cultural specificities of religion and secularisation around the world. For Spohn, processes of secularisation and desecularisation occur in their specific cultural contexts. He argues that, just as no single master narrative can explain the historical and social trajectory of all nations, no single master narrative can explain changes in religiosity in all nations. For this reason, Spohn argues, a theory of secularisation wherein modernity requires religion to dissolve in order to give way to secular understandings of the nation is demonstrably mistaken. Instead, he states that an understanding of multiple modernities highlights the possibility for modern nations to define themselves by religion, just as they can define themselves by secularism.

The Plan of This Book

In the next three parts, I draw on the synthesised definition of secularisation outlined above to analyse key issues at three distinct periods of Australian educational history. Each part provides an account of the key literature and examines two case studies that reveal the complexity of Christian and secular

---

35   Martin, 'Secularization', 465.

36   Adam Possamai, 'Post-Secularism in Multiple Modernities', *Journal of Sociology* 53, no. 4 (2017): 822–35; Willfried Spohn, 'Multiple Modernity, Nationalism and Religion: A Global Perspective', *Current Sociology* 51, no. 3–4 (2003): 265–86.

relationships in education within a similar period. Part 2 focuses on the first two decades of the twentieth century. It explores the meaning of 'free, secular, and compulsory' education in Australia and the relationship between this edict and the presumption of shared Christianity. Part 3 focuses on the 1960s and 1970s, a time of significant change and upheaval in the relationship between Christianity and schooling in realms such as science and social studies not only in Australia but internationally. This was also the period during which federal funding to private, religious, schools, known as 'state aid' was introduced, creating one of the pillars of the faith/state relationship in contemporary Australian education. Part 4 focuses on the twenty-first century, exploring how the Christian faith enters and plays a role within contemporary state-based education. Finally, the conclusion serves as a brief endnote to the work, drawing together the findings from the literature and original case studies.

Part 2: Religious Instruction and State Schools: Expansion and Constraint in the Early Twentieth Century

Introduction

The nineteenth-century 'secular settlements' in the Australian colonies have been, as Jackson identifies, a dominant focus of historical analyses of the relationship between Christianity, secularism, and schooling in Australia.[37] There has been, however, considerable disagreement as to what the nature of these settlements was, and the extent to which they were ever intended to be 'secular' in the contemporary sense of the word. This part begins by examining the literature on early secular education in the Australian context before narrowing in on two early twentieth-century case studies which highlight the extent to which the ongoing effects of these settlements were contingent upon the extent to which it was possible to imagine proponents of religious incursions into state schooling systems as sharing the moral and religious values of the broader community.

The first case study examines the success of the Bible in State Schools campaign in overturning the legal requirement for education in Queensland to

---

37   Carden, 'Bibles in State Schools'; Chavura, "'… but in Its Proper Place…." Religion, Enlightenment, and Australia's Secular Heritage'; Jackson, "'Not in the Business of Indoctrination'"; Low, 'Secularism, Race, Religion and the Public Instruction Act of 1880 in NSW'; Low, 'A Genealogy of the Secular versus Religious Schooling Debate in New South Wales (Part 1)'; Low, 'A Genealogy of the Religious versus Secular Schooling Debate in New South Wales (Part 2)'.

be secular. I have previously identified this campaign as an instance in which imagined representations of a "straight movement directly from religiosity to secularism" are "problematized by historical fact."[38] Similar observations have been made in other contexts. For example, Freathy, examining the record in England, suggests that education for citizenship is often, inaccurately, represented as having progressed from a focus on religious education initially to focus on education for secular citizenship.[39] In the present work, however, I use the case to develop a stronger understanding of how debates over the meaning and use of the word 'secular' influenced policy change in twenty-first-century Australian education and the role of Protestant cultural dominance in determining the outcomes of those debates.

In the second case study, I focus on the closure of a unique form of religious education – the 'German schools' run by German-speaking members of the Lutheran and Apostolic faiths in specific parts of Queensland.[40] This closure, which was justified by authorities on the basis of equal treatment before the law, demonstrates the limits of shared Protestantism in the context of international tensions. It further highlights the significance of research suggesting that secular ideals can act to marginalise racialised 'others.'[41]

"Free, Secular, and Compulsory" Education in Australian History

The definition and nature of a secular schooling system has been a point of contention both in public policy debates and in historical and sociological research. Cathy Byrne notes that, in Australian schooling, "[s]emantic debates about the word 'secular' determine its interpretation and application."[42] In

---

38   Carden, 'Bibles in State Schools', 16.

39   Rob Freathy, 'The Triumph of Religious Education for Citizenship in English Schools, 1935–1949', *History of Education* 37, no. 2 (March 2008): 295–316, https://doi.org/10.1080/00467600701429030.

40   Clarissa Carden, '"A Constant Menace to British Interests": Changing Attitudes towards "German Schools" during World War I', *History Australia* 16, no. 2 (3 April 2019): 324–37, https://doi.org/10.1080/14490854.2019.1590147.

41   Low, 'Secularism, Race, Religion and the Public Instruction Act of 1880 in NSW'; Catherine Connell, 'Contesting Racialized Discourses of Homophobia', *Sociological Forum* 31, no. 3 (September 2016): 599–618, https://doi.org/10.1111/socf.12265; Sindre Bangstad, 'The Morality Police Are Coming! Muslims in Norway's Media Discourses', *Anthropology Today* 27, no. 5 (2011): 3–7; Egbert Ribberink, Peter Achterberg, and Dick Houtman, 'Secular Tolerance? Anti-Muslim Sentiment in Western Europe', *Journal for the Scientific Study of Religion* 56, no. 2 (2017): 259–76.

42   Catherine Byrne, '"Free, Compulsory and (Not) Secular": The Failed Idea in Australian Education', *Journal of Religious History* 37, no. 1 (March 2013): 20, https://doi.org/10.1111/j.1467-9809.2011.01163.x.

Australia, historical ambiguity about the definitions of the words 'secular' and 'religious' has been complicated by a lack of an established church which, according to Melleuish, has contributed to a situation in which:

> There has always been a measure of religious pluralism combined with a measure of indifference, which means that no religious group can monopolise the public sphere. Under these circumstances, it is possible to have a public sphere that is both secular, in the sense that it is free of the dominance of a particular religion or version of a religion, and religious, in the sense that it is informed by the religious values of those who participate in it.[43]

Debates about the meaning of the term 'secular' were pivotal to the different relationships between religion and State education across the Australian states. Hastie suggests that "the majority of education historians exploring this topic have cautioned that the term essentially meant 'non-sectarian,' and that a modern liberal humanist meaning of 'secular' tends to confuse our interpretation of the original intent."[44] A similar suggestion is evident in Chavura's examination of the historical case of Robert Lowe, a nineteenth-century campaigner for secular education in New South Wales. Lowe's arguments against denominational education, and in favour of a secular general system, were positioned "in terms of the good of general Christianity instead of any denominational advantage."[45] In their book *Reason, Religion and the Australian Polity: A Secular State?* Chavura, Gascoigne, and Tregenza say of early 'secular settlements' in Australia that:

> Ideally speaking, to the extent that Australians tended to consider religion as instrumental to the realisation of the state's secular aims, they tended to affirm the secular state's obligation to protect and encourage religion as the surest means of obtaining its secular aims of social peace

---

43 Gregory Melleuish, 'A Secular Australia? Ideas, Politics and the Search for Moral Order in Nineteenth and Early Twentieth Century Australia: A Secular Australia?', *Journal of Religious History* 38, no. 3 (September 2014): 401, https://doi.org/10.1111/1467-9809.12076.

44 David Hastie, 'The Latest Instalment in the Whig Interpretation of Australian Education History: Catherine Byrne's JORHArticle "Free, Compulsory and (Not) Secular": "Secular" in Australian Education History', *Journal of Religious History* 41, no. 3 (September 2017): 387, https://doi.org/10.1111/1467-9809.12386.

45 Chavura, "'... but in Its Proper Place....'' Religion, Enlightenment, and Australia's Secular Heritage', 360.

and prosperity. In other words, most colonials envisioned a *Christian* secular state and education system.[46]

Yet this recognition does not necessarily apply in the same way to all Australian colonies, and its consequences were not felt in the same way in all Australian states. Much research on secular settlements in the Australian states and colonies have focused on New South Wales at the expense of other approaches to determining what a secular school system might look like.[47] The Queensland experience offers a useful comparison point but has been the subject of comparatively little scholarly attention.[48] As I have written elsewhere:

> In Queensland, secular had been interpreted as 'non-religious.' This meant that religion was excluded from the State school curriculum. Ministers of religion were permitted to use school buildings to provide instructions to pupils of their denominations, but this could only occur outside of school hours. In New South Wales secular had been interpreted differently. It was taken to mean 'non-denominational' rather than 'non-religious.'[49]

Ironically, it was the strict, and more modern, definition of 'secular' applied in Queensland which ultimately contributed to the removal of the term from the state's laws and the creation of a system which was free and compulsory, but *not* secular, as will be identified in the first case study of this part.

Remy Low has powerfully challenged the idea that the 'secular' in education is a neutral ideal, using the case of the institutionalisation of the "secular principle" in New South Wales education in the nineteenth-century as an example of how "the secular is always a historically contingent political arrangement inflected by relations of power insofar as it necessitates the regulation of bodies, practices and the lives of people considered religious" and of "how this regulation overlaps historically with the racialisation of those very bodies, practices, and lives; and how this regulation is legitimated in the name of 'citizenship'

---

46 Chavura, Gascoigne, and Tregenza, *Reason, Religion, and the Australian Polity*, 9.

47 Byrne, "'Free, Compulsory and (Not) Secular'"; Chavura, "'… but in Its Proper Place….' Religion, Enlightenment, and Australia's Secular Heritage'; Hastie, 'The Latest Instalment in the Whig Interpretation of Australian Education History'; Low, 'A Genealogy of the Secular versus Religious Schooling Debate in New South Wales (Part 1)'; Low, 'A Genealogy of the Religious versus Secular Schooling Debate in New South Wales (Part 2)'; Low, 'Secularism, Race, Religion and the Public Instruction Act of 1880 in NSW'.

48 Byrne, *Religion in Secular Education*; Carden, 'Bibles in State Schools'; Carden, 'Turning Points'.

49 Carden, 'Bibles in State Schools', 19.

in 'the nation.'"[50] The second case study in this part, that of German schools, offers an important example of how race and religion can come to intersect in educational settings and can lead to the exclusion of groups who do not, or can no longer, fit within the confines of what is imagined to be conventional and included in social orders: a group who, as Low identifies, are deserving of greater consideration in accounts of the role of the secular in education.[51]

Case Study 1: Shared Christianity and the Introduction of Religious Instruction to Queensland State Schools

From 1875, Queensland's system of education was legally free, secular, and compulsory.[52] While this theoretically put it in line with other Australian colonies, its interpretation of the word 'secular' was unusual. A competing, and well-understood, interpretation of what a secular school system looked like could be found in the neighbouring colony of New South Wales. Here, the "*Christian* secular" education system which Chavura, Gascoigne, and Tregenza suggest was preferred by most colonists was in place. Remy Low describes the conditions leading up to the creation of that state's "secular" schooling settlement as follows:

> [T]he shift towards the political institution of a state-run liberal and secular education can [...] be seen a driven, in last part, by a dominant Protestant-liberal populism. For against the background of the Fenian terror scare of the late-1860s and the populist Protestant ferment that followed, the 1880 Public Instruction Act cannot be adequately understood apart from Protestant-liberal demands for a secular education run by the state and a desired elimination of Catholic education as a potential locus of sedition.[53]

Low describes the Act as historically significant because it created a system of education whereby secular, state-funded education stood against a pre-existing religious education system now predominantly run by the Roman Catholic Church. He suggests that not all forms of religion, or all forms of Christianity, could operate within the "secular" context. Indeed, Low argues that the Act

---

50 Low, 'Secularism, Race, Religion and the Public Instruction Act of 1880 in NSW', 173.

51 Ibid., 175.

52 Craig Campbell, 'Free, Compulsory and Secular Education Acts', Dictionary, Dictionary of Educational History in Australia and New Zealand, 1 March 2014, http://dehanz.net.au/entries/free-compulsory-secular-education-acts/.

53 Low, 'A Genealogy of the Religious versus Secular Schooling Debate in New South Wales (Part 2)', 58.

served to generate and perpetuate "hegemonic definitions of what constitutes 'acceptable' religious education that stands alongside secular education under the governance of the nation-state."[54]

In New South Wales, after the passage of the 1880 *Public Instruction Act*, four hours of each school day were to be devoted to secular instruction. One hour could be set aside for religious instruction. This instruction was provided by clergymen to the children of their denominations. The definition of secular instruction was not the same one used in Queensland. In New South Wales the relevant legislation read:

> In all schools under this Act the teaching shall be strictly non-sectarian but the words "secular instruction" shall be held to include general religious teaching as distinguished from dogmatical or polemical theology and lessons in the history of England and in the history of Australia shall form part of the course of secular instruction.[55]

Parents in the New South Wales system could opt out of both general and denomination specific religious instruction for their children. In Queensland, there was no such provision for religious instruction. The relevant legislation included, but did not define, the word secular, and some sections of the Act suggested that religious presence of any kind was unwanted in schools. School buildings, for example, could be used with the permission of the Minister for Public Instruction, the headteacher and the school board outside of school hours for "any lawful purpose other than the holding of religious services."[56] Yet, despite the apparently radical secular orientation of the Queensland school system, Ministers were allowed to provide religious instruction to the children of their denominations at prescribed times outside of school hours.[57] This suggests both recognition of the social importance of Christian religious belief, and an attempt to accommodate this belief within the confines of an avowedly secular system of education. The arrangement, which may be regarded as a compromise, did not satisfy the proponents of religious education and few Ministers took up the opportunity.

---

54 Ibid., 54.

55 New South Wales, 'An Act to Make More Adequate Provision for Public Education' (1880), sec. 7.

56 Queensland, 'Education Act Regulations' (1875), sec. 12.

57 Ibid., sec. 5.

The option to provide religious education outside of school hours was certainly insufficient for the Bible in State Schools League, who would quickly emerge as the most ardent campaigners in favour of introducing religious instruction. For the League and its supporters, the New South Wales system became the preferred model of secular education. From 1890 through to 1910, the League campaigned for changes to education regulations and practice in Queensland to allow for religious instruction to be provided. Their efforts culminated in a successful statewide referendum in 1910 and the passage of the *State Education Acts Amendment Act* of 1910, which removed the word "secular" from the *State Education Act* and allowed for specific forms of religious instruction. Table 3 outlines key moments in their successful campaign.

TABLE 3   Key moments in the history of the Bible in State Schools League

Date	Event
1875	*Queensland State Education Act* (1875) makes state schooling in Queensland free, secular, and compulsory.
1890	Queensland Bible in State Schools League formed.
July 1902	Bible in State Schools League held a mock referendum, purporting to show that a majority of Queensland parents wanted the New South Wales system of religious instruction.
1906	A Bill to provide for a referendum on religious instruction in state schools was put before Parliament. It did not proceed past the second reading.
1908	A Bill to provide for a referendum on religious instruction in state schools was again put before Parliament. This Bill was successful.
13 April 1910	The referendum was held at the same time as the 1910 Federal election. The majority of voters elected to introduce religious instruction to state schools.
24 November 1910	The *State Education Acts Amendment Act* (1910) was assented to. Under this legislation, the word 'secular' was removed from the *State Education Act*. The reading of selected Bible verses in schools was permitted, and ministers of religion were allowed to provide instruction during school hours.

The Bible in State Schools League and its supporters argued that the use of the word 'secular' employed in New South Wales was the correct one. It argued for the New South Wales system of religious instruction to be brought into Queensland schools. This meant that it argued for non-denominational religious teaching to be provided by state school teachers, and for Ministers of Religion (not explicitly, but practically, limited to Protestant Christian clergy) to be permitted to enter schools within class hours to provide lessons to members of their denominations. While the League's position was at odds with the existing 'settlement' in Queensland, what it sought was not necessarily out of keeping with the intentions of the legislators who passed the initial 'free, secular, and compulsory' legislation in Queensland. In 1873, Charles Lilley, who, as Premier in 1870, spearheaded the move to make Queensland the first Australian colony to provide free education, championed a bill, which included in its preamble, the statement that education should be "religious where parents shall not expressly forbid it, but in all respects of such a character that all Christians may receive it without offence and without prejudice to the conscientious convictions of any parent."[58] This provision, however, was removed in the eventual 1875 Act.[59] In a speech introducing the new education provisions, Lilley stated that the legislation would have the effect of "making Queenslanders an intellectual, moral, and religious people [...] unless the churches of the colony altogether fail in their duty."[60]

The education system envisaged by Lilley was intended to ensure that all Queenslanders enjoyed equal access to schooling, which would fit them for their duty in the world. The idea of a secular education system was sold, in part, as a means through which moral, religious, presumably Christian, citizenry could be created. This shows that actions that explicitly differentiated between religious and secular spheres of government operation were nonetheless, at this period in Queensland history, justified in relation to an assumed shared Christianity. Lilley's use of this religious justification suggests that he assumed that many voters viewed the world from a Christian perspective. It also indicates that the religious plurality existing between Christian denominations

---

58   Charles Lilley, 'The New Education Bill of 1873 with the Speech of Mr Lilley in Explanation of Its Provisions Delivered in the Town Hall, Brisbane', in *The New Education Bill of 1873 with the Speech of Mr Lilley in Explanation of Its Provisions Delivered in the Town Hall, Brisbane* (Brisbane: The Courier, 1873), 7.

59   Queensland Government, *State Education Act of 1875* (Brisbane: Government Printer, 1880), sec. 7.

60   Lilley, 'The New Education Bill of 1873 with the Speech of Mr Lilley in Explanation of Its Provisions Delivered in the Town Hall, Brisbane', 16.

was not viewed as precluding a shared understanding of how children ought to be raised and trained.

However, the imagined shared Christian belief system operated in a context of Protestant hegemony. While Australia may not have had a state church, it *did* have a dominant faith group, with the assorted Protestant denominations significantly outnumbering Catholics and those of other or no faiths. The 'secular' principle in New South Wales is generally attributed to that state's *Public Instruction Act* of 1880. This legislation, Low suggests, was based on a Protestant, predominantly middle-class, consensus which excluded Catholics, particularly Irish Catholics. As such, Low argues that "far from being the 'neutral' solution to sectarian conflict, [the Act] was in fact a weapon of it forged in the furnace of the racialisation of Irish Catholicism and ethno-nationalist anxieties about its presence in the colony."[61]

In this context, it is unsurprising that, in Queensland, some of the most prominent defenders of the stricter interpretation of the term 'secular education' were Catholic members of parliament. One example is the Catholic Labour party member Joe Lesina, who was one of the most outspoken opponents of the referendum on religious instruction. During the debate on the second reading of the *Religious Instruction in State Schools Referendum Bill* 1908 (QLD), Lesina made his position clear, stating that: "I have not the slightest sympathy with this attempt or any similar attempt which may be made now or hereafter, to split up our education system by this devious method."[62] In the same debate he highlighted concerns about sectarianism, and appealed to an assumed common understanding of religious plurality, as in the following:

> [If the referendum passes] [t]he Government will have to introduce a Bill to carry out the wishes of the people, and they will have to decide what particular religion shall be taught in the State schools. Of course, the assumption is that they will introduce lessons which will be of no sectarian colour; but who is to be the judge of these matters? If you once call in a majority of people to judge on these matters, then you compel the minority to put up with the decision of the majority on religious questions. You have no right to do that.[63]

---

61   Low, 'Secularism, Race, Religion and the Public Instruction Act of 1880 in NSW', 177.

62   in Queensland Government, *Official Record of the Debates of the Legislative Council and of the Legislative Assembly during the First Session of the Seventeenth Parliament*, vol. CI, Queensland Parliamentary Debates (Brisbane: Government Printer, 1908), 403.

63   In ibid., CI:405.

Lesina's arguments evidence a concern that, in the context of religious plurality, a referendum on a religious issue is inherently inequitable. If the referendum were successful, the Government would be in a position whereby it would be required to choose a form of religion to be taught. Lesina went further, suggesting that even the act of holding the referendum would be unjust. Lesina suggested that there were diverse religious perspectives in Queensland, stating of the referendum that "you are taking the money to hold this referendum out of the pockets of those who have no creed whatever; you are taking it out of the pockets of Jews, Mahommedans, and every other creed."[64] Taxpayer money, from this perspective, could not rightly be spent on anything relating to religion, including a referendum on a religious question. Religious issues were, in Lesina's argument, positioned as outside the usual secular scope of government, and therefore, not issues on which a referendum is reasonable or just. Lesina was equally opposed to the provision of government funds to any religious group for educational purposes, and argued, as did many other opponents, that allowing state schools to provide religious instruction would inevitably lead to state funding being provided to denominational schools:

> If this referendum is carried in favour of having religious instruction in our State schools, you cannot refuse to give grants to the Roman Catholic schools, who provide their own schools without any assistance from the Treasury. It is because of that very fact that I am opposed to this. I am opposed to the State money being used for teaching religious lessons in State schools. I am a secularist, I say that our system of education should be free, compulsory, and secular.[65]

Lesina's arguments suggest a concern that providing religious instruction would alter state schools irreparably, turning them into quasi-denominational schools. In describing himself as a secularist, Lesina claimed an identity opposed to religious instruction which was not, however, opposed to religion itself. This identity was, however, quite distinct from one associated with the "*Christian* secular state" which has been described as shaping particularly nineteenth-century Australian debates.[66]

The supporters of the Bible in State Schools League and their campaign to introduce Christian religious instruction to Queensland state schools

---

64   Ibid., CI:406.

65   Ibid.

66   Chavura, Gascoigne, and Tregenza, *Reason, Religion, and the Australian Polity*, 9.

included members of most Protestant denominations, notably Anglicans and Methodists.[67] They also included many newspapers, including *The Brisbane Courier* (now *The Courier-Mail*). The opponents, on the other hand, included religious groups such as Roman Catholics, Seventh Day Adventists, and some Congregationalists, alongside the Labour Party and such labour-oriented newspapers as *Week*, *Truth*, and *Worker*.[68] While some opponents in Parliament claimed a 'secularist' identity, there was no clear secularist lobby involved in the debate, and even those who described themselves as 'secularist' were clear that they were not opposed to religion. The conflict was not one between non-believers and Christians. It was primarily between Protestants who viewed faith as an indispensable part of moral education, on the one hand, and Catholics, allied with other groups who viewed religious instruction as an inappropriate use of state-funded school time, on the other. This distinction appears to lend credence to the assertion, made by opponents of the League, that religious instruction in state schools could lead to sectarian divisions.

The means through which the Bible in State Schools League was able to promote its messages demonstrates the privileged position of Christianity in Queensland. Local newspapers reported on sermons preached in major churches. The Bible in State Schools League used this prominent social position as a means of spreading their message through arranging for ministers of the various member denominations to preach sermons on the value of religious education in schools.[69]

In 1902, when the Bible in State Schools League arranged a mock referendum to bring their cause "before the public,"[70] newspapers such as *The Brisbane Courier* provided them with legitimacy. This referendum, unofficial and non-binding as it was, was nonetheless a significant undertaking. Garland indicated that 20,942 parents were found to be in favour of Bible reading and religious instruction, while 1,417 were not. *The Brisbane Courier* reported on a meeting held after the referendum, which showed that a majority of parents supported the aims of the League. Its report presented the results of the

---

67   Yvonne Perkins, 'Queensland's Bible in State Schools Referendum 1910: A Case Study of Democracy' (Honours, Sydney, University of Sydney, 2010), 6.

68   Perkins, 'Queensland's Bible in State Schools Referendum 1910: A Case Study of Democracy'.

69   E.g. 'Bibles in State Schools: Sermons on Sunday', *The Telegraph*, 27 July 1981, 3.

70   DJ Garland, 'The Bible in State School League', 1910, OM66-05/5 Bible in State Schools League, Queensland Records 1890–1915, Queensland Records, John Oxley Library, State Library of Queensland, Australia.

referendum as a victory, and as an accurate representation of community sentiment.[71]

In 1906, Premier William Kidston introduced a Bill to provide for a referendum on the subject of the introduction of religious instruction and Bible reading to state schools. This Bill passed the second reading stage but was not taken any further. A Bill was again introduced in 1908 – it was this that passed and provided for the referendum. This Bill required the electors of Queensland to vote on the question of religious instruction in state schools during the 1910 Federal election. Voters were asked to respond to the following question:

> Are you in favour of introducing the following system into State schools, namely: –
>
> The State schoolmaster, in school hours, teaches selected Bible lessons from a reading-book provided for the purpose, but is not allowed to give sectarian teaching;
>
> Any minister of religion is entitled, in school hours, to give the children of his own denomination an hour's religious instruction on such day or days as the school committee can arrange for;
>
> Any parent is entitled to withdraw his child from all religious teaching if he chooses to do so.

Slightly over half of eligible voters, 53.29%, took part in the referendum.[72] Of this percentage 74,228 electors voted 'Yes,' 56681 voted 'No,' and there were 7,651 informal votes. Despite the arguments, examined later in this part, of parliamentarians who pledged to oppose this alteration to the school system, the *State Education Acts Amendment Act* (1910) was passed based on this result. This legislation explicitly removed the word 'secular' from the existing legislation.[73] Children could, in theory, experience an entirely secular education due to a provision in the legislation that allowed parents to withdraw their children from religious instruction. This was an opt-out, rather than an opt-in, provision. This provision endured until 2006, when the regulations were clarified to ensure that children were sent to religious instruction only if their parents nominated a denomination of instruction, denoting an active choice

---

71   'Bibles in State Schools: The Recent Referendum. Large "yes" Majority. Meeting in Centennial Hall', *The Brisbane Courier*, 8 July 1902, 5.

72   Queensland Government, *Official Record of the Debates of the Legislative Council and of the Legislative Assembly during the First Session of the Seventeenth Parliament*, C1:478.

73   Queensland, 'State Education Acts Amendment Act' (1910), sec. 2.

to participate.[74] The legislation passed in 1910 provided that primary school teachers could read selected non-sectarian Bible lessons to pupils and allowed Ministers of Religion to enter schools to teach the children of their denomination, on a day appointed by a school governing body. Parents and guardians were entitled to withdraw children from all religious instruction by notifying the headteacher of their wish to do so.[75]

While religious instruction, provided by clergy (or later, their representatives) became an important feature of state education in Queensland, non-sectarian Bible lessons did not, although they would later be integrated into the Civics and Morals curriculum.[76] This appears to have been due to the resistance of teachers. The specially prepared Bible Readers, which were introduced in 1916, tended to remain untouched, with headteachers failing to enforce Bible teaching among their staff.[77] The fate of the school Bible Readers – some of which, Spaull and Sullivan state in their history of the QTU, were found years later, unopened – demonstrates the power of a group whose voices were too often ignored in parliamentary debates and newspaper columns – the teachers.[78]

A Case of Desecularisation?
The case of the Bible in State Schools League, and the introduction of religious instruction to state schools, highlights the significance of Chavura's argument that 'religious' and 'secular' ideals have not always been oppositional in Australian history.[79] In this case, two competing ideas about the definition of the term 'secular' existed within a single Australian state. The definition of the word 'secular,' and the legitimate relationship of the state to the majority religion, came into conflict with the school as the battleground on which the differences were played out. Interestingly, the problem of definition was

---

74   Queensland, 'Education (General Provisions) Regulations' (2006), sec. 29, https://www
     .legislation.qld.gov.au/LEGISLTN/CURRENT/E/EducGenPrR06.pdf.
75   Queensland, State Education Acts Amendment Act, 1910, sec. 2.
76   Clarissa Carden, 'Reading to the Soul: Narrative Imagery and Moral Education in Early to
     Mid-Twentieth Century Queensland', in *Sight, Sound and Text in the History of Education*,
     ed. Jody Crutchley, Stephen Parker, and Sian Roberts (Abingdon, Oxon; New York, NY:
     Routledge, 2019), 119–34; Clarissa Carden, 'Reading to the Soul: Narrative Imagery and
     Moral Education in Early to Mid-Twentieth Century Queensland', *History of Education* 47,
     no. 2 (2018): 269–84, https://doi.org/10.1080/0046760X.2017.1420242.
77   DC McDiarmid, 'Religious Education in Queensland State Schools: 1860–1972' (Grad. Dip.
     R.E., Brisbane, Mount Gravatt College of Advanced Education, 1987), 16.
78   Andrew Spaull and Martin Sullivan, *A History of the Queensland Teachers' Union* (Sydney:
     Allen & Unwin, 1989).
79   Chavura, '"… but in Its Proper Place.…" Religion, Enlightenment, and Australia's Secular
     Heritage'.

not settled. While the forces who saw 'secular' as potentially encompassing religious practices were successful in obtaining their desired social change, the removal of the word 'secular' from the legislation governing education in Queensland suggests that the word retained its previous definition and remained understood as antithetical to religion.

A key dimension of the theory of secularisation outlined in this text is that it is situated in broader power relations. At this moment in history, Queensland was predominantly Protestant. The "structures of power and webs of culture"[80] created a situation in which a referendum on the question of religious instruction could be passed through Parliament, put to the people of Queensland, and resolved in favour of Christian ideals. Byrne has argued that the introduction of Christianity to Queensland state schools was a key desecularising moment in the state's history.[81] However, this moment instead brought to prominence the existing religiosity of the Queensland voting base. While the incident does highlight the problems with the presumption of linear narratives whereby institutions, including schooling systems, become more secular with modernisation, it predominantly served to reinforce an existing Protestant hegemony. This hegemony was already, as the League had pointed out, expressed through approved lessons. In this sense, the removal of the 'secular' principle in Queensland created an education system that was secular in the same sense as that in New South Wales, in that it was shaped and influenced by the presumption of a shared Protestant Christianity.[82]

The voices of teachers are largely absent from the available historical record. Their actions, however, speak to a conflict between their position as professional educators and the new subject they were expected to teach. The fact that the Bible Readers appear, in some cases, to have been largely unused indicates that the integration of the Bible into state school classrooms, the aspect of the altered legislation which speaks most strongly to a reduction of the level of differentiation between religion and school environments, could only be achieved with the cooperation of classroom teachers. This demonstrates the problem with analyses of secularisation which focus solely on the power of the state. While the state had the power to mandate that religious instruction should occur, teachers had agency, and could, in their classroom practices, resist the outcome of the referendum.

---

80   Martin, 'Secularization'.

81   Byrne, *Religion in Secular Education*, 220.

82   Hastie, 'The Latest Instalment in the Whig Interpretation of Australian Education History'; Byrne, "'Free, Compulsory and (Not) Secular'"; Low, 'Secularism, Race, Religion and the Public Instruction Act of 1880 in NSW'.

SECULARISATION IN AUSTRALIAN EDUCATION SINCE 1910

Despite this, the introduction of religious instruction to state schools high-lights the changing and recursive nature of secularisation in Queensland's history. Queensland's state schools, between 1875 and 1910, were, to a limited extent, secular archipelagos, to adapt Wilford's term.[83] In the context of an environment which was defined both by high rates of Protestant beliefs and sectarian conflicts, state schools had been constituted as non-religious spaces. This specific secularised space underwent its own process of desecularisation or resacralisation as a result of the actions of a highly motivated and influential group.

Case Study 2: German Schools and the Limits of Shared Christianity

From the late nineteenth-century, pastors of the German Apostolic and Lutheran churches in Queensland began opening 'German schools,' which operated on one day per week and allowed for the teaching of religious faith alongside the German language. Children attending these schools received most of their education in the state school system. The existence of German schools was first seriously challenged in 1912, and they were made to cease operating entirely in 1915.

The case of the Bible in State Schools League was an instance in which Protestant Christian dominance in Queensland state schooling was revital-ised and reconfirmed. This case, however, demonstrates the limitations of Protestant Christian identity as a source of power and influence in educational decision-making during the early part of the twentieth century. In particular, it highlights the tensions involved when loyalties to state, nation, and empire are pitted against loyalties to a shared religious faith. It also demonstrates that an issue that may be rightly understood as religious by one group, can also, simultaneously, and based on equally strong reasoning, be considered secular. Together, these case studies highlight the contradictory processes of seculari-sation and desecularisation, and the complex relationships between religious communities and state education, which existed in the early twentieth cen-tury. In focusing on a change which related to a single ethnic and religious group who had already been marked out as a wartime enemy, it exposes the uneven terrain of conflicts between Christian and secular ideals in Queensland education, demonstrating that these conflicts and their outcomes are always dependent upon a range of external factors.

Through the mid to late nineteenth century, German Lutheran congre-gations attempted to set up parish schools in Queensland, as in the other Australian states. According to the Lutheran pastor and historian F Otto

83   Wilford, 'Sacred Archipelagos', 328–48.

Theile, these schools, which taught in both English and German, did not provide students with the knowledge they needed to compete in the workforce. Specifically, young people who attended Queensland Lutheran schools did not graduate with the English language skills required to participate fully in Queensland society. Theile writes that, to serve the best interests of students, the parish schools were closed and pastors took on the work of teaching children in German and religion on one day of each week.[84]

The provision of religious instruction in this way ensured that Lutheran children could attend state schools without missing out on the preparation viewed as necessary to become fully-fledged adult members of the church. The Lutheran church was able to cede authority to the state, to mark a clear space between religious and secular instruction, without ceding the right to provide their own education. According to Williams, by 1909, only one Lutheran school

TABLE 4   Major events in the closure of German schools

Date	Event
Late 1890s–c. 1909	Lutherans of German origin in Queensland closed their parish schools and opened 'German schools' to run alongside the state schooling system.
9 January 1912	*State Education Acts Amendment Act* (1912) was assented to. This legislation made attendance at state schools compulsory on all school days.
July 1912	The Secretary for Public Instruction refused to count attendance at 'German schools' toward the average attendance in calculating teacher payments.
4 August 1914	Britain entered WWI against Germany and Australia followed.
January 1915	Queensland Teachers Union resolved that students should not be permitted to be absent from school to attend German schools.
1915	Department of Public Instruction informs German pastors that students are no longer permitted to be absent from state schools to attend German schools.

84   F Otto Theile, *One Hundred Years of the Lutheran Church in Queensland* (South Brisbane: Publication Committee of the Queensland District United Evangelical Lutheran Church in Australia, 1938), 88.

in Queensland operated on five days per week, with twenty-one operating once per week, and two operating fortnightly.[85] This is in contrast with the system Meyer describes in the southern Australian states, where Lutherans, like Catholics, viewed education and faith as inseparable, and for this reason, saw private, denominational schooling as an essential part of keeping the faith.[86]

The continuation of German schools in Queensland was first seriously challenged in January of 1912, with the passage of the Queensland *State Education Acts Amendment Act*. This Act replaced the clause in the previous legislation requiring students to attend on one-half of all school days, each half year. Instead, it stated:

> The parent of every child of not less than six nor more than fourteen years of age shall, unless some valid excuse exists, cause such child to attend a State school or Provisional school each day on which such school is open in each half-year.[87]

School attendance had been mandatory since 1900, but the previous compulsion clause only required that children attend school on half of the days on which it was open each half year. Children were, therefore, able to attend to other commitments, including paid employment, domestic chores, and religious responsibilities. Under these circumstances, German schools had been able to operate during weekdays without breaching any laws.

The changes to the *Education Act* met with concern from the Queensland German Lutheran community, even before they were passed. For example, on December 11, 1911, F Otto Theile, of Bethania Junction, in his capacity as a pastor and as Secretary of the United German and Scandinavian Lutheran Church, wrote to AJ Thynne, Member of the Legislative Chamber, in reference to the then-proposed legislative changes. Theile wrote that "what makes this provision very irksome is the fact that the Act asks of all children to attend absolutely on every day the school is open for tuition." He objected on two bases: firstly, because some families in his parish relied on their children for domestic support and assistance, and secondly, due to the interference this clause would

---

85   Glen Leslie Williams, 'The German Language and the Lutheran Church in Queensland', *Queensland Heritage* 2, no. 8 (1973): 33.

86   Charles Meyer, "'What a Terrible Thing It Is to Entrust One's Children to Such Heathen Teachers": State and Church Relations Illustrated in the Early Lutheran Schools of Victoria, Australia', *History of Education Quarterly* 40, no. 3 (2000): 302, https://doi .org/10.2307/369555.

87   Queensland, 'State Education Acts Amendment Act' (1912), sec. 8.

cause with religious education. He added that "we can not allow that such an Act should hinder us in the execution of our religious duties."[88]

Theile's assertion that he and his parishioners "can not allow" legislative interference "in the execution of our religious duties," is suggestive not only of the significance of German schools to his congregation but also of his certainty that, in his position as a Christian pastor, he could expect to be heard. Theile's position was supported at the time by the Department of Public Instruction. Attendance at a German school was accepted, after the passage of the Act, as a valid reason for non-attendance at state schools. The means through which this was accomplished, however, created dissent among teachers.

Students were permitted to attend German schools, but where they did so, they were marked as absent on the attendance roll of their state school. Given that teachers' salaries were based on average attendance, the regular absence of German students from the state school classroom had a significant impact on the income of teachers working in predominantly German districts. This issue was raised at the 1912 Queensland Teachers' Conference. The conference declared that, as attendance at technical classes allowed pupils to be marked as being in attendance, children who missed school due to attendance at German schools, should be recorded in the same way.[89] A deputation of teachers brought their concerns concerning this matter to the Secretary for Public Instruction, the Hon. K. Grant, in July 1912. According to *The Brisbane Courier*, Grant informed the teachers that, as German schools were not under state control, attendance at such schools could not be accepted as attendance at state schools.[90] This meant that pupil attendance at German schools, like attendance at technical schools, would continue to impact teacher pay. In January 1914 the conference again resolved "[t]hat attendance at German schools should be reckoned as attendance at State schools."[91] Again, this change did not occur.

By 1915, teachers had stopped requesting that attendance at German schools be counted as attendance at state schools to calculate their income. Instead, they sought to have attendance at German schools prohibited for state school students altogether – a position that was quickly taken up by the Department

---

88 F Otto Theile, 'F. Otto Theile to Hon. AJ Thynne: On an Act to Amend the Education Act', 11 December 1911, 1–2, Item ID 1623127, Queensland State Archives, http://www.archives search.qld.gov.au/Search/ItemDetails.aspx?ItemId=1623127.

89 'Teachers' Conference', *Darling Downs Gazette*, 11 January 1912, 5.

90 'Teachers' Needs: Deputation to the Minister. A Promise of Betterment', *The Brisbane Courier*, 15 July 1912, 10.

91 'Teachers' Conference: Registration of Schools. Appeal Board Question. The Training College', *The Brisbane Courier*, 15 January 1914, 8.

SECULARISATION IN AUSTRALIAN EDUCATION SINCE 1910

of Public Instruction. In mid-1915, the Department produced a document listing the twenty-one German schools operating in Queensland and informed the pastors of these schools that they were required to close.[92] While reports continued to trickle in of students absenting themselves from state schools to attend German schools,[93] by 1916, the Department claimed that German schools no longer existed.[94]

A range of factors contributed to the closure of German schools. Their continued official acceptance in the immediate period post-1912, when the change in legislation would have justified their closure, suggests that there was a willingness, on the part of the state government, to facilitate the needs of Christian groups. By 1914, however, non-religious principles, including the pressures and prejudices associated with the war, the fact that teachers were paid based on average attendance, and, potentially, a belief in the benefits of sustained attendance at state schools, all served to render German schools undesirable and deviant. The religious aspect of these schools – their primary purpose – was rarely prominent in arguments over their continued place in society. Where this was brought up and emphasised, it was by the Lutheran pastors themselves. There appears, then, to have been a disconnect in the way this issue was perceived, with Lutheran pastors viewing it as a religious issue, and other key players, such as teachers, considering the subject in relation to non-religious concerns, including wartime enmity and economic interests.

Faith, the 'Secular' Principle, and Minority Culture:
Relationships in Early Twentieth-Century Schooling

From 1914, the Great War changed how people of German descent living in Queensland were represented and responded to across a range of spheres, including in relation to religion and education.[95] A group that had previously enjoyed certain privileges, including the right to self-determination and

---

92   Department of Public Instruction, 'German Schools: Summary Showing Names of Schools and Names and Addresses of German Pastors Notified of Departmental Decision in This Matter', 1915, Item ID 1623126, Queensland State Archives.

93   J Old, 'Letter from the Inspector of Police, Maryborough to the Under Secretary Department of Public Instruction Regarding Children Not Attending Binjour Plateau State School', 28 June 1915, Item ID 1623128, Queensland State Archives, http://www.archivessearch.qld.gov.au/Search/ItemDetails.aspx?ItemId=1623128.

94   John Douglas Story, 'JD Story to EM Land: Re. German Schools', 11 June 1916, Item ID: 2036412, Queensland State Archives, http://www.archivessearch.qld.gov.au/Search/ItemDetails.aspx?ItemId=2036412.

95   Bruce Pennay, 'An Australian Berlin and Hotbed of Disloyalty: Shaming Germans in a Country District during Two World Wars', Journal of the Royal Australian Historical Society 92, no. 1 (2006): 15; RJW Selleck, '"The Trouble with My Looking Glass": A Study of the

control in areas such as the upbringing of children, and the maintenance of culture, found itself the subject of suspicion and distrust.[96] It was as a result of this change in social status that, only a few years after the victory of the Bible in State Schools League, the relationship between religion and the state in the schooling sector was again contested and redefined.

Where the Bible in State Schools League redefined the existing secular system of state education for all children, the banning of German schools impacted a relatively small and homogenous group. German schools provided religious instruction to the offspring of German-speaking adherents to certain denominations of the Christian faith. German schools were a means of retaining German culture and religious faith primarily associated with Lutherans; however, they were also run by the Apostolic church in Queensland, founded by Rev Niemeyer. Niemeyer had previously been a member of the Lutheran church, and many of his adherents were former Lutherans.[97] While the German schools were generally viewed as being associated with the Lutheran church, Niemeyer was one of the most vocal proponents of the continuation of these schools. The two groups were often conflated in relevant public discourse, with 'Lutheran' being used as a denominational description for all of the churches associated with German schools. The practice of running German schools appears to have been well established by 1912, when adjustments to the compulsory education requirements first brought it into question.

While the nature of German schools in Queensland was atypical, German Lutheran congregations throughout Australia took on the work of creating religious schools. Hatoss notes that across South Australia, Victoria, and New South Wales, sixty bilingual Lutheran schools were in operation by 1916, with 49 in South Australia.[98] Unlike Queensland's German schools, these bilingual schools provided a general, as well as a religious, education, and their students did not rely on the state system. Hatoss' research suggests that while these schools initially provided instruction only in German, with English taught

---

Attitude of Australians to Germans during the Great War', *Journal of Australian Studies* 4, no. 6 (June 1980): 2–25, https://doi.org/10.1080/14443058009386804.

96 Gerhard Fischer, *Enemy Aliens: Internment and the Homefront Experience in Australia, 1914–1920*, UQP Paperbacks. Australian History (St Lucia, Qld., Australia: Portland, Or: University of Queensland Press; Distributed in the USA and Canada by International Specialized Book Services, Inc, 1989); Jenny Tilby Stock, 'South Australia's 'German'Vote in World War I', *Australian Journal of Politics & History* 28, no. 2 (1982): 19.

97 CM McGrath, 'Heinrich Friedrich Niemeyer: Foundation Leader of the Apostolic Church of Queensland', *Queensland History Journal* 23, no. 3 (2016): 189.

98 Aniko Hatoss, 'Language, Faith and Identity: A Historical Insight into Discourses of Languge Ideology and Planning by the Lutheran Church of Australia', *Australian Review of Applied Linguistics* 35, no. 1 (2012): 101.

as a second language, social and political pressures led to a decrease in the amount of German taught. By around 1914, English was the dominant language of instruction in many such schools.[99] This is in stark contrast to the German schools of Queensland, where language and faith were taught together.

Queensland was different in other ways. Hatoss' research also suggests that, by 1913, the Lutheran church in Australia was concerned with the question of language. In congregations across the country, including in Queensland, pastors were performing their duties in both German and English due, in part, to a preference of young people for the English language.[100] The Church feared that a transition to English, as the primary language of worship, could lead to a loss of theological knowledge and faith, but holding this against the danger of losing young believers, opted to make the transition. There was therefore already a strong movement within the Lutheran church in Australia, to adapt to English language usage by the time the First World War broke out. However, Williams states that by 1913, only fifteen of the nearly seventy Lutheran congregations in Queensland held a service in English every month.[101]

Queensland, by 1911, had the second-highest German population in Australia. This population has been described as scattered, unlike the German communities of South Australia.[102] Despite the dispersal of this population, small communities were formed in which German Lutherans were able to retain some of the traditions of their forebears. Before the First World War, Queensland's population of German Lutherans was situated in its southeast, around the cities of Ipswich and Toowoomba.[103] By the war, then, German immigrants to Queensland largely lived in more or less concentrated settlements. At this time, the Lutheran church in Queensland was overwhelmingly the German church, and the isolation of German immigrants from native English-speakers meant the German language would be used in their communities.[104] Some important figures in Queensland played a role in ensuring that the German language would remain a central part of Lutheran identity. German pastor F Otto Theile, who was born in South Australia, but underwent his ministry training in Germany, has been described as "a man feeling completely German," who viewed the German language and German identity as necessarily connected

---

99   Ibid.
100   Hatoss, 'Language, Faith and Identity: A Historical Insight into Discourses of Language Ideology and Planning by the Lutheran Church of Australia'.
101   Williams, 'The German Language and the Lutheran Church in Queensland', 32.
102   Stock, 'South Australia's 'German' Vote in World War I'.
103   John Frank Williams, *German Anzacs and the First World War* (Sydney: UNSW Press, 2003), 17.
104   Williams, 'The German Language and the Lutheran Church in Queensland', 31–32.

to Lutheranism.[105] The German schools described in this part were, therefore, a uniquely Queensland invention, emerging from the coalescence of the lack of success of more traditional Lutheran private schools, the relative isolation of German communities from native English-speakers, and the presence of strong religious figures who saw Lutheranism and the German language as inextricably linked.

The closure of German schools fits into a broader pattern of anti-Germanism in Australia during the war. This has been explored, at length, by scholars such as Fischer, Moses, and Williams.[106] The impact of prejudice against people of German extraction in both the first and second world wars was often expressed in extreme prejudice towards Australia's Lutheran population.[107] Hatred of German nationals during the war was such that Germans were re-raced. Whereas before the wars Germans were conceived of as white, warfare transformed them into an ethnic other.[108]

A Case of Secularisation?

The Australian Census of 1910 revealed that 94.6% of Queenslanders adhered to some form of Christianity, as did 95.9% of all Australians.[109] This case, therefore, occurred at a period during which the overwhelming majority of Australians, including the vast majority of Queenslanders, identified with some form of the Christian faith. It was therefore possible, and indeed plausible, for Lutheran pastors to appeal for special consideration based on their shared faith with the Queensland people as a whole. However, the Australian home front during the First World War was one in which populations became

---

105   Christine Winter, 'Inter-War Transformation of German-Australian Identity: The Case of Queensland Pastor Friedrich Otto Theile', in *Germans in Queensland* (Peter Lang Publishing, 2012), 138.

106   Fischer, *Enemy Aliens*; John A Moses, 'The University of Queensland's Official Reaction to the Great War, 1914–15', *Queensland History Journal* 22, no. 9 (2015): 664–76; Williams, *German Anzacs and the First World War*.

107   Elizabeth Koepping, 'Hidden Damage and Current Needs: Pulpit and Pew in Lutheran Australia', *Scottish Journal of Theology* 60, no. 04 (November 2007), https://doi.org/10.1017/S0036930607003742.

108   e.g. Emily Robertson, 'Norman Lindsay and the "Asianisation" of the German Soldier in Australia during the First World War', *The Round Table* 103, no. 2 (4 March 2014): 211–31, https://doi.org/10.1080/00358533.2014.898505.

109   GH Knibbs, 'Census of the Commonwealth of Australia Part 4. Religions', Census Report (Canberra: Department of Home Affairs, 1911), http://www.ausstats.abs.gov.au/ausstats/free.nsf/0/B8982A23D75F18B6CA2578390013015D/$File/1911%20Census%20-%20Volume%20II%20-%20Part%20VI%20Religions.pdf.

SECULARISATION IN AUSTRALIAN EDUCATION SINCE 1910

fractured along the lines of national, rather than religious, identity. Gerhard Fischer writes that:

> The Australian story of the home front war offers a sobering counter projection to the story of the heroic Anzacs overseas. While the Australian soldiers at Gallipoli are said to have discovered their mateship and loyalty to each other as defining features of their sense of self, Australians at home were encouraged by their government to 'dob in' their German Australian neighbours who had been their mates only a few weeks earlier. Many did so with great enthusiasm, driven by an exaggerated fear for their country's safety, but also by a felt need to become involved in an adventurous mission: to participate in the affairs of the world from which the isolated colonial outpost of the British Empire had been largely excluded in the past.[110]

In this context, appeals to Christian tradition could not overcome the competing loyalties of both individuals and government authorities to the state, the nation, and the British empire. This was further problematized by the existence of legal provisions for ministers of religion to enter schools to provide religious instruction. To a lesser extent, the claims of pastors like Niemeyer to be teaching morality and values such as loyalty were contradicted by the fact that, since 1905, the Queensland school curriculum had included the explicit teaching of secular civics and morals.[111]

Karel Dobbelaere's notion of organisational secularisation offers a useful means of understanding the process undergone by the Lutheran church in Queensland during this time. Organisational secularisation for Dobbelaere occurs when, "[c]onsciously or unconsciously, and quite often by force of circumstance, churches and denominations adapt to the secularised world."[112] In this case, the German Lutheran and Apostolic churches were made, by force of

---

110   Gerhard Fischer, "'Negative Integration' and an Australian Road to Modernity: Interpreting the Australian Homefront Experience in World War I', *Australian Historical Studies* 26, no. 104 (April 1995): 224, https://doi.org/10.1080/10314619508595974.

111   Carden, 'Reading to the Soul: Narrative Imagery and Moral Education in Early to Mid-Twentieth Century Queensland', 2019; Carden, 'Reading to the Soul: Narrative Imagery and Moral Education in Early to Mid-Twentieth Century Queensland', 2018; Kelsey Halbert, 'History Teaching and the Values Agenda' (PhD Thesis, Townsville, James Cook University, 2009), 28; Peter Meadmore, 'The Introduction of the "New Education" In Queensland, Australia', *History of Education Quarterly* 43, no. 3 (2003): 372–92.

112   Dobbelaere, *Secularization*, 123.

circumstance, and against their inclinations, to forgo an established religious practice and adapt to the intrusion of additional external control. In doing so, these churches were forced to cede some of the authority they held over the children of their denominations. This authority had been extensive when compared to that held by some other Christian denominations, in part, due to the relationship between the faith itself and the position of Queenslanders of German origin, as a minority culture and language group.

One of the causes of organisational secularisation is that conventional religions have to take on a wider social purpose for being which causes them to lose their operative status.[113] In this case, the religion had already taken on a wider, negative, social function without this being its intention or consent. It became a symbol of German incursion into Australia. German Lutheranism represented a potential threat from within. German schools became a dangerous space in which radicalism and anti-Australian attitudes could be developed. While the explicit denial of the right of German parents to educate their children in their faith and language was all but impossible, the removal of accommodations, previously granted, served as an impediment to exercising this right. For this reason, the operative status of the Lutheran church was challenged.

It is, therefore, important to recognise that what was, for one group, an external removal of religious authority was, for the majority, a means of addressing an existential threat. In the face of this threat, the bid of a Christian denomination to educate its children was rejected. It is worth bearing in mind that this was more or less contemporaneous with the victory of the Bible in State Schools League. In terms of impact, the two cases were quite different. The Bible in State Schools League secured a change in state education that impacted all state schools more or less equally, though, of course, the geographical location of a particular school, and the denomination to which children belonged, would affect this. The banning of German schools, however, impacted only the members of a relatively socially and geographically contained group. Where the former case expanded the rights of Protestant Christian groups marginally and solidified the position of Christianity in society, the latter significantly disrupted and altered one particular minority group. The desecularisation which appears to have occurred during the previous case, therefore, does not appear to have been widespread, to the extent that educational authorities respected Christianity generally.

---

113   Ibid., 113.

The closure of German schools confined Lutheran education to the Sunday Schools and to the regular religious instruction which could be provided, due to the actions of the Bible in State Schools League, by visiting clergymen – the proviso, in this latter case, being that such instruction must be conducted in English. There was thus a tension between individual parishioners and a church organisation, which viewed the role of the church in educating the young as a vital one, and a state which saw its authority as central, particularly where there was a risk of young people being taught to be disloyal to Australia and to Britain.

This case reveals the extent to which the definition of an issue or practice as 'Christian' or 'secular' in nature, is historically, culturally, and geographically situated. German schools could be understood as a 'Christian' practice where no competing narratives or loyalties were in play. As in the previous case, the "structures of power and webs of culture" in operation at this historical moment and geographical location are extremely important in understanding the outcome of this case.[114] Before the war, German Lutheran and Apostolic congregations could align themselves with the Christian majority. As Christians, they were able to seek special consideration, which allowed them to entrust the secular component of their children's education to the state while retaining the right to impart Christian knowledge in the manner and language they chose. Once Britain, and by extension, Australia, was at war with Germany, the 'Christian' aspect of Lutheran and Apostolic identities became subordinate to the 'German' aspect of their identities. As Germans, these congregations were viewed with suspicion, and their special privileges were revoked.

Conclusion

This part has examined some of the tensions which emerged in relation to the 'free, secular, and compulsory' system of education in place in early twentieth-century Australia. While previous scholarship has rightly identified contestations over the meaning and implementation of the term 'secular' as a key focus for examination, this part has also demonstrated that secularisation itself – the extent to which a religious group could claim authority over the education system as a whole – was inconsistent, contested, and unevenly experienced. The use of secularisation theory in this context raises questions about individual and family choices concerning schooling and the extent to which dominant religious groups should have power over curricula. These

---

114   Martin, 'Secularization', 465.

questions continue to resonate today. They are taken up again in the next part through an examination of the complex culture wars of the 1960s and 1970s.

Part 3: Government and Non-government Schools: Questions of Faith, Choice, and Control in the 1960s and 1970s

Introduction

The previous part focused on the interpretation of the word 'secular' in Australian systems of 'free, secular, and compulsory' education, highlighting, through two state-specific case studies, the extent to which the meaning and significance of 'secular' schooling differed according to broader political and other needs. This part moves forward several decades, to examine contentions that arose in Australian education funding and practice through the 1960s and 1970s, and which are inextricably connected to broader, transnational but particularly Anglosphere, movements and issues.

The 1960s have been recognised as a key moment in the decline of Christian power in the West.[115] According to McLeod, "it is clear that this decade marks in some important respects a turning point in Western religious history."[116] Yet, as he recognises, the precise nature of this turning point remains a matter of contention. It is not the intention of this part to take a stance on this debate. Rather, this part contributes to knowledge of the Australian debates which occurred alongside fervent debates about the role of Christianity in schooling elsewhere.[117]

While the 1960s and '70s saw increased dissension over Protestant domination about schooling choices in Australia, there was still a sense in which imagined shared Christian identities – including, but not necessarily equivalent to, shared Protestant identities – were present in decision-making. Stephen Jackson notes that most of the scholarship on secular and religious tensions in Australian education "focuses on the secular settlements created in the mid-to-late-19th century during the foundational moments of Australian mass schooling" and argues for the significance of the 1960s through to the 1980s as a time of additional "Australian educational secular settlements"

---

115   E.g. Callum G Brown, *The Death of Christian Britain: Understanding Secularisation, 1800–2000*, 2nd ed, Christianity and Society in the Modern World (London; New York: Routledge, 2009).

116   McLeod, 'The Crisis of Christianity in the West', 327.

117   Rob Freathy and Stephen G Parker, 'Secularists, Humanists and Religious Education: Religious Crisis and Curriculum Change in England, 1963–1975', *History of Education* 42, no. 2 (March 2013): 222–56, https://doi.org/10.1080/0046760X.2012.761733.

deserving of consideration.[118] Writing on a debate over the reform of religious education in South Australia in the 1970s, Jackson identifies the perplexing suggestion, by various Christian churches, that the programme should not proselytise, but should nonetheless be "distinctively Christian."[119] This type of suggestion made sense within the context of a society that could comfortable describe itself as Christian, although, as the German schools case study highlights, belonging to the category 'Christian' relied on other social factors. However, there was sufficient pushback to see decisions made by governments to the benefit of religious schools, or religious intervention in public schools, as potentially controversial. In this part, I map some of the key debates of the period, before providing two case studies – the introduction of federal government funding to private religious schools throughout Australia, and the banning of *Man: A Course of Study* (MACOS) and the *Social Education Materials Project* (SEMP) in Queensland. These cases highlight the extent to which the outcomes of tensions between Christian and secular impulses were, and are, dependent upon both international circumstances and individual leadership.

Public Funding and Christian Schools

One of the key spheres in which Christianity interacts with primary and secondary education in Australia is through fee-charging private religious schools. These schools are maintained, not only by the contributions of parents but also by government funding. The extent to which governments ought to dispense funding to private schools, and how this funding should be distributed, remains a key area of debate in Australian education. The focus in this part is on the specific debates of the 1960s and 1970s when federal government funding for these schools was first offered. These debates are significant, not just in and of themselves, but because of the effect on the nature of education in Australia today.

The firmly established practice of funding private schools has contributed to a situation in which parents frequently choose religious schools for non-religious reasons. For example, Caldwell holds that private schooling is popular in twenty-first-century Australia for primarily pragmatic, rather than ideological, reasons, mainly attributable to the widely-held perception that private schools provide a better education than government schools.[120]

---

118   Jackson, "'Not in the Business of Indoctrination'", 250.

119   Ibid., 254.

120   Brian J Caldwell, 'Is Private Schooling Becoming the Preferred Model of School Choice in Australia?', *Journal of School Choice* 4, no. 4 (7 December 2010): 378–97, https://doi.org/10.1080/15582159.2010.526840.

Similarly, Bouma argues that that Australian parents perceive faith-based schools as offering better opportunities for advancement and university admission. However, he indicates that the values and discipline associated with these schools are also important factors in their popularity. From this perspective, private schools, including Catholic schools, are popular not because they are religious, but because government schools are seen as academically or socially inferior.[121] Research exploring how these schools represent themselves supports the argument that the perceived academic, social, and personal benefits of private schooling are central to the appeal for parents. For example, Meadmore and Meadmore, drawing from a study of thirty Australian private schools, argue that elite private schools engage the discourse of "emotional intelligence," to present their religious pastoral care programs as an essential part of the development of a well-rounded child.[122] Similarly, Wardman et al. demonstrate that the prospectuses of elite Australian schools for girls feature nostalgic images of innocent femininity.[123] These schools position themselves as places in which girls will develop emotional competence and become 'well rounded' young women.

An additional factor contributing to the popularity of private schooling is a perception that private schools instil 'values,' broadly and vaguely defined, in their students. The 'values' debate does not rest on the interests of the specific faith groups which operate schools but rather serves to position private (largely Christian) schooling in opposition to public schooling. Maddox identifies that this perception became particularly politically potent between the mid-1990s and early 2000s. Maddox describes an "Australian values debate" whereby then-prime minister John Howard remarked that the state system was "too politically correct" and lacked "traditional values."[124] This discussion was associated with the provision of additional federal funding for the establishment of a large number of new Christian schools.[125] The Australian experience is similar to a phenomenon that occurred at around the same time

---

121 Gary D Bouma, *Australian Soul: Religion and Spirituality in the Twenty-First Century* (Cambridge, UK; New York: Cambridge University Press, 2006), 160.

122 Daphne Meadmore * and Peter Meadmore, 'The Boundlessness of Performativity in Elite Australian Schools', *Discourse: Studies in the Cultural Politics of Education* 25, no. 3 (September 2004): 375–87, https://doi.org/10.1080/0159630042000247944.

123 Natasha Wardman et al., 'Starry Eyes and Subservient Selves: Portraits of "Well-Rounded" Girlhood in the Prospectuses of All-Girl Elite Private Schools', *Australian Journal of Education* 54, no. 3 (2010): 249–61.

124 Marion Maddox, *God under Howard: The Rise of the Religious Right in Australian Politics*, 1st ed (Crows Nest, NSW: Allen & Unwin, 2005), 185.

125 Maddox, *God under Howard.*

in England, wherein former Prime Minister Tony Blair encouraged the proliferation of faith-based schools.[126] The political encouragement of faith-based schools is, therefore, a transnational movement within which Australia figures.

Within Australia, the proliferation of new Christian schools, as a result of increased funding, was justified by appeals to diversity and choice. Maddox argues that Australian school funding "perversely exacerbates" both financial and ideological privilege, through funding even very wealthy private schools and those which teach anti-government sentiments.[127] In justifying their access to such funding, Maddox finds, Christian schools represent themselves "simultaneously as guardians of unassailable mainstream values (and therefore deserving state support), and a beleaguered minority in a hostile, secular world (and therefore deserving state protection)."[128] She describes a policy that allows a school sector to claim both of these positions to be "a very curious cultural policy indeed."[129]

Elsewhere, Maddox notes that parents without specific religious commitments, who choose to send their children to Christian schools to obtain 'values,' may be unaware of the specific strands of Christian belief that are taught.[130] She describes the rise of themelic schools, Protestant private schools which derive much of their funding from government sources, and which are not 'branded' in the same way as Catholic, government, or elite schools. Maddox argues that these schools are problematic in that they can provide science teaching which goes against scientific consensus, assert the superiority of divine law to the laws of the state, and engage in discrimination based on sexuality, beliefs, and other factors. She indicates that representatives of themelic schools, alongside prominent Christian lobbyists, claim to speak for all Christians. However, she states that "they in fact represent only one narrow segment of the followers of Jesus Christ, who also include representatives of longstanding progressive traditions with a conscientious openness to other beliefs."[131]

---

126 Geoffrey Walford, 'Faith-Based Schools in England after Ten Years of Tony Blair', *Oxford Review of Education* 34, no. 6 (2008): 689–99.

127 Marion Maddox, 'Are Religious Schools Socially Inclusive or Exclusive? An Australian Conundrum', *International Journal of Cultural Policy* 17, no. 2 (March 2011): 170–86, https://doi.org/10.1080/10286632.2010.544729.

128 Ibid., 184.

129 Ibid.

130 Maddox, 'Are Religious Schools Socially Inclusive or Exclusive?'.

131 Marion Maddox, 'The Church, the State and the Classroom: Questions Posed by an Overlooked Sector in Australia's Education Market', *UNSWLJ* 34 (2011): 314–15.

Similarly, Symes and Gulson state that the philosophies underpinning some fundamentalist private schools "are far from benign and are part of a full-blown crusade against contemporary, secular society that is being played out in the politics of Australian education."[132] The authors contend that these schools, which fit into the non-elite, Protestant, themelic mould described by Maddox[133] opened in large numbers in New South Wales in the late 1990s and early 2000s. In their view, the fact that these schools can open in areas already well-served by government schools is the result of parental anxieties about the quality of education and discipline in government schools. They charge low fees and are tailored to be affordable for parents in outer metropolitan areas who wish to buy into private education. The concerns highlighted by Symes and Gulson about the tensions between the ethos of some religious schools, and the norms of the contemporary Australian state, have often come to the fore when religious schools have sought to be exempted from non-discrimination laws. From a legal perspective, Evans and Ujvari argue that religious schools "are deserving of some protection of their distinctive worldview, but such protection is nonetheless consistent with the idea that they should be subject to more aspects of discrimination law than is currently the case in Australia."[134] Offering a different take on this issue is Mortensen, who indicates that, in Queensland, debates over the right of religious schools to discriminate against LGBTIQ people in de facto relationships, are not merely about the collision of religious freedom and equal opportunity.[135] Instead, he argues that the government funding of religious schools renders the question equally one of distributive justice. He suggests that religious schools should be free to accept government funding, but that such funding should only be provided if schools agree not to discriminate. This idea is founded on the assumption that taxpayers should not be made to fund religious schools that are permitted to discriminate when such discrimination would otherwise contravene Australian law. In proposing such an alteration to the funding arrangements, Mortensen implicitly suggests that, as religious schools are funded due to their secular utility, such funding should only be provided if the religious function of the schools does not hinder the secular function of education.

---

132 Colin Symes and Kalervo Gulson, 'Crucifying Education: The Rise and Rise of New Christian Schooling in Australia', *Social Alternatives* 24, no. 4 (2005): 23.

133 Maddox, 'The Church, the State and the Classroom'.

134 Carolyn Evans and Leilani Ujvari, 'Non-Discrimination Laws and Religious Schools in Australia', *Adelaide Law Review* 30 (2009): 56.

135 Reid Mortensen, 'A Reconstruction of Religious Freedom and Equality: Gay, Lesbian and De Facto Rights and the Religious School in Queensland', *Queensland University of Technology Law and Justice Journal* 3, no. 1 (2003).

Overwhelmingly, contemporary contentions about the nature of funding for religious private schools begin with the presumption that such funding is, to one degree or another, necessary or inevitable. The normalisation of government funding for private schooling, and its justification on bases that are not explicitly religious, renders the specific context in which it initiated less visible. However, as Campbell and Sherington state, federal funding for both government and non-government schools in Australia occurred in the context of "revived debate over state aid for Catholic schools, the establishment of the Democratic Labor Party and other Cold War pressures."[136] These external situational factors, explored in this part, can shine a more complex light on a development that undoubtedly benefited established, predominantly Christian, religious groups.

Social Science and Humanities Education and the Christian Right

As with the relationship between the government and religiously-run private schools, the position of social science and humanities education at a primary and secondary level remains a source of contention. As the next part will demonstrate, concerns about teaching related to LGBTIQ issues, in particular, have arisen as twenty-first-century preoccupations of some conservative commentators and members of the Christian Right in Australia.[137] Social studies curricula, in particular, came to the attention of the Christian Right within the Anglo-American world alongside the development of what has been described as the New Social Studies movement in the 1960s and 1970s. Part of this movement was the project *Man: A Course of Study*, also known as MACOS, which originated in the United States, where it was contested by the Christian Right.[138] The development of new forms of social studies which more closely mirrored academic disciplines has been linked, in the United States, to the Cold War, and concerns about the quality of American education as compared to that of the USSR.[139] In the second case study in this part, I describe how a dominating religious campaigner, facilitated by an unusually receptive state

---

136   Craig Campbell and Geoffrey Sherington, *The Comprehensive Public High School Historical Perspectives* (Basingstoke: Palgrave Macmillan, 2013), 68.

137   Carden, "'Fiddling with Young Kiddies' Minds'"; Jay Daniel Thompson, 'Predatory Schools and Student Non-Lives: A Discourse Analysis of the Safe Schools Coalition Australia Controversy', *Sex Education* 19, no. 1 (2 January 2019): 41–53, https://doi.org/10.1080/14681 811.2018.1475284.

138   Paul G Fitchett and William Benedict Russell, 'Reflecting on MACOS: Why It Failed and What We Can Learn from Its Demise', *Paedagogica Historica* 48, no. 3 (June 2012): 469–84, https://doi.org/10.1080/00309230.2011.554423.

139   Ibid., 471.

Premier, was able to contribute to the banning of MACOS and the unrelated SEMP suite of resources.

It is important to note, though, that the success of campaigns against the content of education is often difficult to judge. For example, McGeorge, writing on two campaigns against teaching evolution in New Zealand's primary schools, identifies that seemingly successful protests in the 1940s scarcely "made any appreciable difference to the way in which science and nature study were taught in New Zealand schools."[140] Similarly, the success of the campaign against MACOS and SEMP in Queensland was only partial and did not result in a ban on these programmes in private schools or, importantly, a change in teacher attitudes.

Case Study 3: The Introduction of Federal Funding for Religious Schools

The 1961 Australian Census showed that 88.3% of Australians were Christian, with 24.9% of that group identifying as Catholic. In 1966 the figures had moved to 88.2% and 26.2% respectively.[141] Christianity, and particularly Protestant Christianity, had, since the period covered in the previous part, lost some of its dominance, but the number of people identifying as Catholics had increased. Catholic children predominantly attended non-government Catholic schools. However, there was no uniform process of providing government funding to these schools, and no government funding at all on a federal level, Schools relied on parental contributions through fees and donations. As a result, the Catholic education system was experiencing financial pressure throughout Australia.

In July 1962, Bishop John Cullinane, of the diocese of Canberra-Goulburn, closed the six Catholic schools of Goulburn, New South Wales, for six weeks. As a result of this, 2000 students attempted to enrol in their nearest government schools. This action was made in protest over the New South Wales State Government's insistence that improvements be made to a local Catholic school which could not be managed with the funds available. A total of 640 Catholic students were enrolled in state schools, but the remainder could not be accommodated. While most students returned to their schools on July 22, around

---

140   Colin McGeorge, 'Evolution and the New Zealand Primary School Curriculum 1900-1950', *History of Education* 21, no. 2 (June 1992): 205, https://doi.org/10.1080/0046760920210207.

141   Australian Bureau of Statistics, 'Chapter – Religious Affiliation', 20 January 2006, http:// www.abs.gov.au/ausstats/abs@.nsf/46d1bc47ac9d0c7bca256c470025ff87/bfdda1ca506d-6cfaca2570de0014496e!OpenDocument.

10% remained in the public system.[142] This enrolment was not, for most families involved, intended as a long-term solution to the funding pressures upon Catholic schools, but, instead, was a short-term action to draw attention to the need for assistance. At the time this was a state, not a Commonwealth, issue.[143] However, it became an issue relevant to the two major Australian political parties, the Labor and Liberal parties, from the 1950s. During the mid-1950s, a split occurred in the Labor party, leading to the formation of a third party, the Democratic Labor Party.[144] This new party was supported by Catholics, and the issue of state aid was important to their base. In this context, the Liberal party, under the stewardship of Prime Minister Robert Menzies, could secure the support of the traditional voting bases of both the Labor and Democratic Labor parties by supporting state aid.[145]

Complicating the context was the international political situation of the Cold War. As a Prime Minister, Robert Menzies was deeply concerned with the possibility of the Cold War breaking out into an active and devastating conflict. This concern played an important role in his actions as Prime Minister leading, for example, to his opposition to the 1953 Convention on Peace and War, because of his fear that it was supported or run by communists.[146] For Clark, the circumstances of the Cold War, and particularly the launching of Sputnik, created an increased impetus for Menzies to fund science education in Australia.[147] The provision of funding for non-government schools was introduced in the context of an expansion in university enrolment, and funding alongside increasing public concern for equity in access to education.[148]

---

142   John Warhurst, '50 Years since Australia's "Most Poisonous Debate"', *Eureka Street* 22, no. 13 (8 July 2012), http://www.eurekastreet.com.au/article.aspx?aeid=32230.

143   Ibid., 75.

144   Michael Lyons, 'Defence, the Family and the Battler: The Democratic Labor Party and Its Legacy', *Australian Journal of Political Science* 43, no. 3 (September 2008): 425–42, https://doi.org/10.1080/10361140802267233.

145   Jennifer Clark, 'In the Shadow of Sputnik: A Transnational Approach to Menzies Support for Science Education in Australia, 1957–1964', *Paedagogica Historica* 53, no. 5 (3 September 2017): 623–39, https://doi.org/10.1080/00309230.2016.1267781.

146   Phillip Deery, 'Menzies, the Cold War and the 1953 Convention on Peace and War', *Australian Historical Studies* 34, no. 122 (October 2003): 248–69, https://doi.org/10.1080/10314610308596254.

147   Clark, 'In the Shadow of Sputnik'.

148   Hannah Forsyth, 'Expanding Higher Education: Institutional Responses in Australia from the Post-War Era to the 1970s', *Paedagogica Historica* 51, no. 3 (4 May 2015): 379, https://doi.org/10.1080/00309230.2014.929592.

TABLE 5   Key moments in the introduction of state aid for private schools

Date	Event
1963	During the campaign for the 1963 federal election, Prime Minister Robert Menzies announced his intention to begin funding science facilities in secondary schools – both government and non-government.
25 June 1964	*States Grants (Science Laboratories and Technical Training)* (1964) was assented to, allowing the Federal Government to provide grants to the states for use in funding science laboratories and other training in secondary schools.
1964	Council for the Defence of Government Schools (DOGS) was founded to oppose funding for non-government schools.
3 December 1968	*States Grants (Secondary School Libraries) Act* (1968) was assented to, allowing the Federal Government to provide grants to the states for use in funding libraries for secondary schools.
1972	The Interim Committee for the Australian Schools Commission was appointed.
May 1973	The report of the Interim Committee for the Australian Schools Commission (the Karmel report) was delivered
1981	DOGS challenge to funding for non-government schools failed in the High Court.

In October 1962, Prime Minister Robert Menzies publicly denied that the Commonwealth Parliament was in talks with the Catholic Church to provide state aid to church schools.[149] In this denial, he suggested that he had no intention to change public policy and introduce state aid. However, during the 1963 election campaign, Menzies stated that "there is a special need for improved science teaching in the secondary schools if we are to keep in step with the march of science."[150] In recognising this need, he promised to

---

149   Robert Menzies, 'Transcript 621 | PM Transcripts', 10 September 1962, https://pmtran scripts.pmc.gov.au/release/transcript-621.

150   Robert Menzies, 'Transcript 853 | PM Transcripts Federal Election 1963 – Policy Speech', 11 December 1963, https://pmtranscripts.pmc.gov.au/release/transcript-853.

SECULARISATION IN AUSTRALIAN EDUCATION SINCE 1910

make available £5 million per year for building and equipment related to science teaching in secondary schools, regardless of whether they were government or non-government schools. Menzies also proposed providing 10000 scholarships per annum to support students in the final two years of secondary school, worth up to £100 per year for fees and books and £100 per year for maintenance. These scholarships would be available at both public and non-government schools.[151] They would not, he warned after his election, be available until at least 1965. Grants for science buildings and equipment would be arranged more quickly. This was the genesis of an approach that would be adopted by subsequent Prime Ministers of Menzies' Liberal party. State and non-government schools were to be treated equally.

The other major political party, The Australian Labor Party, was conflicted over the issue of state aid for denominational schools. At the party's 1963 conference delegates from the states of Western Australia and New South Wales took opposing stances on the question, with the former arguing that all state aid should be banned.[152] The opposing stances may have been associated with different degrees of connection to Catholicism. The New South Wales delegates prevailed, with the party rejecting the idea that state aid should be banned unilaterally.[153] The conference agreed that government aid should be provided to students of private schools but not to the schools themselves.[154] This was the practice in place in Queensland. The effect was that, by the time of the 1963 election, both major parties agreed that some form of funding should be provided by governments to assist with the costs associated with private schooling. State aid was no longer a controversial question. It was a matter of political expediency.

The Cold War context created an incentive, for parties on both sides of the conflict, to invest in scientific education and innovation. After the launch of Sputnik, the United States invested in both formal and informal education efforts to increase public understanding of science and technology.[155] Also in the United States, national funding for scientific education, information, and dissemination led to the creation of a new category of scientist: the "information

---

151 Robert Menzies, 'Transcript 866 | PM Transcripts Broadcast over National Stations – Final Broadcast', 27 November 1963, 866, https://pmtranscripts.pmc.gov.au/release/transcript-866.

152 'Labor Bid for No "State Aid"', *The Courier Mail*, 19 July 1963, State Library of Queensland.

153 'A.L.P. Rejects Schools Aid Ban', *The Courier Mail*, 2 August 1963, 1.

154 'Labor "No" on School State Aid', *The Courier Mail*, 3 August 1963, 3.

155 Anne M Zandstra and J Wesley Null, 'How Did Museums Change during the Cold War? Informal Science Education After Sputnik', *American Educational History Journal* 38, no. 1–2 (2011): 321–39.

scientist."[156] In Australia, the Industrial Fund for the Advancement of Science, a group of businessmen and headmasters of private schools, had already been providing funding for science laboratories in non-government secondary schools by the time Menzies announced that the Federal Government would provide such funding.[157] This group viewed such laboratories as a necessary means of addressing the perceived superiority of the Soviet Union in science education.[158] The fund provided for several science laboratories to be built in Queensland boys' colleges. The focus on boys was intentional – a spokesperson told *The Courier-Mail* that the best results for the money spent would be obtained by focusing on boys as "it is a fact that boys stay at work longer than girls."[159]

The efforts of the Industrial Fund provided part of the impetus for government funding to improve science education in Australia. In 1964 Menzies referred to a representative of the group, Mr Robson, as "my old friend and competitor" and stated that:

> I would like to say that the idea put forward to me and now in the course of being carried out owes not a little to the existence of the Industrial Fund and its imaginative suggestions which entered my mind and the minds of my colleagues.[160]

The provision of early federal funding to both government and non-government secondary schools was therefore influenced by a group that was primarily concerned with supporting non-government, often elite, schools for boys. Funding for school laboratories was provided to the states through direct grants under the *States Grants* (*Science Laboratories and Technical Training*) Act, which was enacted and commenced on June 25, 1964. It provided for payments to be made

---

156   Nathan R Johnson, 'Rhetoric and the Cold War Politics of Information Science', *Journal of the Association for Information Science and Technology* 68, no. 6 (2017): 1375–84.

157   Campbell and Sherington, *The Comprehensive Public High School Historical Perspectives*, 68.

158   Geoffrey Sherington and JP Hughes, "'Money Made Us": A Short History of Government Funds for Australian Schools', in *Controversies in Education: Orthodoxy and Heresy in Policy and Practice*, ed. Helen Proctor, Patrick Brownlee, and Peter Freebody, 2015, 165, http://public.eblib.com/choice/publicfullrecord.aspx?p=1967239.

159   'Industry Promotes Science in Schools', *The Courier Mail*, 5 April 1963, 2, State Library of Queensland.

160   Robert Menzies, 'Transcript 888 | PM Transcripts Opening of New Science Building at Geelong College, Geelong, Victoria – 12th February 1964', 2 December 1964, https://pmtranscripts.pmc.gov.au/release/transcript-888.

to states under the condition that they were used to build secondary school laboratories and to provide science equipment and technical training. The legislation stated that "'school' means a school or a similar institution, whether conducted by a State or not."[161] In the eyes of the Federal Government, government and non-government schools were equivalent in their right to receive funding: a position which was now enshrined in legislation. This was the first time the Federal Government funded a religious education practice, rendering it an important moment in the history of the chaplaincy case study examined in the next part.

The provision of government funding for non-government schools did not go uncontested. The Council for the Defence of Government Schools (DOGS) was founded in 1964 to combat state aid. This organisation acted as a pressure group from 1964 through to 1969, when it became a minor political party, nominating candidates for state and federal elections, until resuming its original function as a pressure group in 1972.[162]

DOGS continues to operate as a secular pressure group that opposes government funding for non-government schools on the basis that it constitutes government support of religion. The group is best known for challenging Federal Government funding to non-government schools in the High Court of Australia in 1981 on the grounds of s.116 of the Constitution of the Commonwealth of Australia, which prohibits a law establishing any religion. Its journey to the High Court was long and arduous and, as an account published by the group in 1981 suggests, filled with frustration at the legal system.[163] The case was decided in 1981 in favour of the Commonwealth.[164] The fact that the financial aid was expressly limited to the educational activities was important in this decision, as was the Court's finding that the funding did not establish a state religion.

In 1968, the Queensland newspaper *The Courier-Mail* reported that Roman Catholic children were still attending state schools, while enrolments at

---

161 Commonwealth of Australia, 'States Grants (Science Laboratories and Technical Training) Act', Pub. L. No. 50 of 1964 (1964), sec. 2(4).

162 Dean Jaensch and David Scott Mathieson, *A Plague on Both Your Houses: Minor Parties in Australia* (St Leonards, NSW: Allen & Unwin, 1998), 10.

163 M. J Ely and Council for Defence of Government Schools (Vic.), *Erosion of the Judicial Process: An Aspect of Church-State Entanglement in Australia: The Struggle of Citizens to Be Heard in the Australian Full High Court on the State Aid Issue, 1956–1980* (Melbourne: Defence of Government Schools, Victoria, 1981).

164 CJ Barwick et al., Attorney-General (Vic); Ex Rel Black v Commonwealth ('DOGS case'), No. 2 (HCA 2 February 1981).

non-government schools remained close to static.[165] Catholic schools, in particular, continued to experience financial problems through the 1960s. At the time, teachers in the Catholic school system received lower salaries than those in the government system. These teachers sought higher pay during the 1960s, producing what *The Courier-Mail* described as "a crisis in the system."[166] A representative of Catholic schools in Queensland stated that increased allowances to non-government schools from the state would solve these problems. Catholic schools, along with a handful of other non-government schools, also opposed a State Industrial Commission ruling that gave male and female teachers equal pay.[167] The Queensland Education Minister told a group of parents in 1968 that his government was leaning toward providing more aid to church schools.[168]

At a 1968 conference in Brisbane, The Australian Teachers' Federation, a national union of teachers, unanimously carried a motion calling for additional government funding for education – something it stated it had been seeking for sixteen years. It also requested federal funding for libraries and teacher-librarians.[169] In the same year, the head of the Roman Catholic teaching order, the De La Salle Brothers, said that the Australian government had offered a significant boost to independent schools through the funding of science laboratories, and that he hoped something similar would be done to develop the humanities "perhaps through libraries."[170] SB Page, Deputy Librarian of the University of Queensland, and Vice-President of the Queensland Branch of the Library Association of Australia, wrote an op-ed in May 1968 promoting school libraries and stating that libraries are "an essential part of the educational apparatus."[171]

These calls for aid did not go unanswered. At the end of 1968, the *States Grants (Secondary School Libraries) Act* was passed.[172] This legislation allowed the Federal Government to give grants to the states to provide libraries and associated materials for both government and non-government schools. In this legislation, as in the earlier legislation which funded science

---

165 'Record Number at School next Week, but Less Pressure', *The Courier Mail*, 25 January 1968, 9.

166 'Teachers' Pay Rise Objection', *The Courier Mail*, 9 March 1968, 7.

167 'Claim Court Erred in Teachers' Equal Pay', *The Courier Mail*, 12 March 1968, 8.

168 'More Help to Church Schools Hinted', *The Courier Mail*, 5 April 1968, 12.

169 'Teachers Push for Education Finance', *The Courier Mail*, 10 January 1968, 3.

170 'More Aid Needed – RC Teacher', *The Courier Mail*, 17 April 1968, 13.

171 SB Page, 'School Libraries Badly Needed in Queensland', *The Courier Mail*, 10 May 1968, 2.

172 Commonwealth of Australia, 'States Grants (Secondary Schools Libraries) Act' (1968), http://www.legislation.gov.au/Details/C1968A00125.

SECULARISATION IN AUSTRALIAN EDUCATION SINCE 1910

laboratories, the word 'schools' was defined as encompassing both state and non-government schools.

The election of Gough Whitlam in 1972 brought a new political party into power. While Whitlam's Labor party had traditionally opposed state aid, under his guidance, it had become a supporter of the principle. One of his first acts as Prime Minister was to institute the Interim Committee for the Australian Schools Commission. Whitlam became Prime Minister on December 5, 1972. The Interim Committee for the Australian Schools Commission held its first meeting on December 21.[173] It was appointed to examine the position of both government and non-government schools in Australia, and to make recommendations on their financial needs and the way their needs should be met.[174]

Whitlam said that the committee was tasked to ensure "that every Australian child who embarks upon secondary education next year [in 1973] will leave school with an equal start in life."[175] The "futile debate on State aid and State rights in education," he said, "is now ended."[176] The Karmel report was delivered in May of 1973. The authors of that report emphasised that the provision of equal funding to non-government schools, regardless of need, had obscured the very real class differences between schools within the non-state sector.[177] The report showed that schools had access to very different resources and that funding should be based on socio-economic need. The Interim Committee which produced this report was a direct precursor to the later Australian Schools Commission.[178]

The recommendations of the Karmel Report were immediately acted upon. Whitlam said that the rapidity of his government's action, in providing an additional $404 million for education in 1973–74, spoke to its "wholehearted commitment to education."[179] The reformed education program meant, he

---

173 Gough Whitlam, 'Transcript 2746 | PM Transcripts Schools Committee – Press Statement', 13 December 1972, https://pmtranscripts.pmc.gov.au/release/transcript-2746.

174 Peter Karmel et al., 'Schools in Australia: Report of the Interim Committee for the Australian Schools Commission' (Canberra: Interim Committee for the Australian Schools Commission, 18 May 1973), iv.

175 Gough Whitlam, 'Transcript 2759 | PM Transcripts Report to the Nation – 20 December 1972', 20 December 1972, https://pmtranscripts.pmc.gov.au/release/transcript-2759.

176 Ibid.

177 Karmel et al., 'Schools in Australia: Report of the Interim Committee for the Australian Schools Commission', 16.

178 Ian Wilkinson, 'State Aid to Non-Government Schools', in *Dictionary of Educational History in Australia and New Zealand*, 5 December 2013, http://dehanz.net.au/entries/state-aid-non-government-schools-2/.

179 Gough Whitlam, 'Transcript 3073 | PM Transcripts Speech by the Prime Minister the Hon. E.g. Whitlam, Q.C., M.P., for the Opening of the Advanced Education, Hobart,

said, that "[a]id will be available to all schools, without distinction, on a 'needs' basis."[180] The Senate, controlled by the Liberal party, did not immediately enact the legislation providing for this new program. The legislation would, as Whitlam told a 1973 press conference, require phasing out of government assistance to a small number of schools, which the report had deemed outside the funding boundaries funding.[181] Whitlam also questioned the arrangements under the previous government, which he said did nothing to "help the establishment of new Catholic schools in growing areas," or "for the training of teachers in existing Catholic schools," and "left existing Government schools as deprived and overburdened as ever."[182] In Whitlam's hands, the division between government and non-government schools was far less significant than the distinction between economically privileged and deprived schools. In delivering his second budget, he noted that "the expected outcry" had not only been in the form of parliamentary opposition but also "the predictable condemnation from the wealthy, the privileged, the richest private schools" and others.[183] State aid had, by this point, become such an established orthodoxy that the decision of Whitlam's Labor government to target it more carefully was controversial.

Government-Supported Faith?

For scholars such as Casanova and Martin, secularisation is dependent on cultural contexts, with very different movements occurring in different national contexts.[184] While the introduction of funding for non-government, religiously motivated schools is a movement which may be read as desecularising, involving as it does a provision of government funding to religious organisations, the circumstances of the decision to introduce state aid refute such a reading.

Sunday 18 November 1973', 18 November 1973, https://pmtranscripts.pmc.gov.au/release/transcript-3073.

180 Gough Whitlam, 'Transcript 3089 | PM Transcripts The First Year', 12 February 1973, https://pmtranscripts.pmc.gov.au/release/transcript-3089.

181 Gough Whitlam, 'Transcript 3093 | PM Transcripts Prime Minister's Press Conference, Parliament House', 12 April 1973, https://pmtranscripts.pmc.gov.au/release/transcript-3093.

182 Gough Whitlam, 'Transcript 3231 | PM Transcripts Speech by the Prime Minister, Mr EG Whitlam QC MP, to an Election Campaign Meeting at Springvale Town Hall, Melbourne, Victoria', 30 April 1974, https://pmtranscripts.pmc.gov.au/release/transcript-3231.

183 Gough Whitlam, 'Transcript 3399 | PM Transcripts Speech by the Prime Minister, Mr EG Whitlam QC MP, at the ALP Regional Council – Townsville', 21 September 1974, https://pmtranscripts.pmc.gov.au/release/transcript-3399.

184 Casanova, 'Cosmopolitanism, the Clash of Civilizations and Multiple Modernities'; Martin, 'Secularization'.

The first such factor is the significance of Catholic schools in campaigning for state aid. They were a large minority faith, not a group with hegemonic power. Unlike Protestants in early twentieth-century Queensland, the Catholics of mid-twentieth century Australia could claim only around a quarter of the population as adherents. Further, as Godfrey and Pouw-Bray argue, the introduction of state aid to private schools came at a moment where Protestant opposition to such funding had become less extreme.[185]

The nature of Catholicism as a faith is also an important element in understanding this case. Berger describes the "fullness" of the Catholic universe, as opposed to the "essentials" of the Protestant.[186] Education remained a sacred part of life, something which rightly fell within the purview of the church, for Catholics, but not Protestants. Dobbelaere has described the tendency of the Catholic church to retain its own education and hospital sectors as a partly failed attempt at insulation.[187] In this case study, the Catholic Church was requesting assistance to allow the continuation of a practice that was deeply associated with its spiritual doctrine. However, as Dobbelaere identified in a study of Catholic subsystems in Belgium, the purpose of a Catholic school or hospital is first and foremost to provide good education or medical care.[188] In this case, the provision of state aid served to ensure that Catholic schools could provide a good education for their students. The aid supported aspects of the school, such as science laboratories and libraries, which could be defined as having a role to play in the provision of education in any school, religious or otherwise. It is possible, then, that state aid, far from allowing Catholic schools to retain their sacred function, ensured that the professionalisation of education within these schools continued to advance, thus further displacing the religious function.

The second significant factor in understanding the extent to which the introduction of state aid to non-government schools was a secularising or desecularising moment is the Cold War context. Clark argues that Menzies' initial decision to fund private schools was not a means of courting the Catholic vote, but was instead a response to the political climate, in which funding for

---

185   John R Godfrey and Alexander Pouw-Bray, "'I Believe in Fair and Bonny Play": David H. Drummond and State-Aid: 1930–1962', *Education Research and Perspectives* 27, no. 2 (2000): 63–74.

186   Peter L Berger, *The Sacred Canopy: Elements of a Sociological Theory of Religion* (Garden City, New York: Anchor Books, 1969), 111.

187   Karel Dobbelaere, 'Professionalization and Secularization in the Belgian Catholic Pillar', *Japanese Journal of Religious Studies* 6, no. 1/2 (1978): 39–64.

188   Dobbelaere, *Secularization*, 46.

science became necessary and desirable.[189] In particular, Russian scientific advances, including the launch of Sputnik, led to an international situation in which scientific literacy was highly prized. She suggests that it was the need for science reform that led to the introduction of state aid.[190] From this perspective, funding for science laboratories is part of a broader, international shift toward prioritising science in the face of highly visible advances in Russian technology.

Another factor in understanding the relationship between this funding and secularisation theory is the language through which funding for non-government schools has been justified. Campbell writes that, by the 1970s, school choice had become understood as the right of Australian citizens.[191] This was a break from the past, wherein families had been discouraged or actively prevented by government regulation from choosing the school their children attended.[192] This discourse of choice was part of the dominant mode of justifying state aid employed by the Prime Ministers examined, and it reflects the significance of the politics of liberalism, including freedom of religion, as part of Western democratic thinking.

These factors suggest that, far from constructing a state religion or otherwise privileging religious faith, the introduction of state aid was a response to non-religious needs. While state aid may have the consequence of supporting religious education, it was not introduced for this purpose, and it was not justified on this basis. Government funding for private education is provided based on the non-religious function of these schools.

Berger, in *The Sacred Canopy*, writes that in a secularised world, religion cannot perform the function of constructing "a common world within which all of social life receives ultimate meaning binding on everybody," but instead becomes limited to segregated and limited enclaves.[193] It is that very limitation and segregation, occurring even within the context of schools run by churches for the children of their members, which renders comprehensible the language of politicians speaking in favour of state aid for religious schools.

---

189 Clark, 'In the Shadow of Sputnik'.

190 Jennifer Clark, 'Taking the Lead in Science Education Reform in NSW, 1957–1964: Wyndham, Messel, Robson and Menzies', *History of Education Review* 44, no. 2 (5 October 2015): 236–52, https://doi.org/10.1108/HER-02-2014-0012.

191 Craig Campbell, 'Changing School Loyalties and the Middle Class: A Reflection on the Developing Fate of State Comprehensive High Schooling', *The Australian Educational Researcher* 32, no. 1 (2005): 19.

192 Craig Campbell, Helen Proctor, and Geoffrey Sherington, *School Choice: How Parents Negotiate the New School Market in Australia* (Crows Nest, NSW: Allen & Unwin, 2009), 2–3.

193 Berger, *The Sacred Canopy*, 134.

The education provided within these schools was not generally lauded for its religious or moral character by politicians, but was, instead, positioned in relation to ideas about what Australian children are entitled to receive by virtue of being Australians. Schooling was viewed as a choice made in the context of the marketplace, with the government being responsible for ensuring that no choice made by parents resulted in an unacceptable level of education being imparted to their children or an unacceptable level of financial burden on the part of parents. The funding that was provided by the Federal Government could not have been as clearly, articulately, and consistently justified, were the educational functions of non-government schools inseparable from their religious functions. None of the politicians who argued for state aid suggested that it was justified based on the religious teachings in non-government schools. Instead, funding was to provide quality education for all Australian children.

This analysis highlights the need for a definition and theorisation of secularisation that is attentive to social context beyond legislative change and figures of church attendance or religious identification. DOGS took a position in line with some secularisation theorists, wherein the separation of church and state is the central or the only factor determining the extent to which a country is secular. From this reading, the introduction of government funding to non-government, predominantly church-operated, schools would constitute a desecularising moment. However, the international context and the arguments used to justify this funding demonstrate the operation of priorities that had little to do with religious belief.

Case Study 4: Banning MACOS and SEMP: A Local Victory for the Religious Right

Broadly, the national landscape through the 1960s and 1970s was one in which Christian, primarily Catholic, groups obtained new rights and recognition in relation to their role in providing primary and secondary education. However, the justification was not religious, and the outcomes of government funding for private schools are more often discussed through the lens of class inequalities than issues associated with the separation of church and state. However, even in a broader context in which religious belief alone was not sufficient to justify a change on a national level, more local conflicts could have quite different outcomes. The banning of MACOS and SEMP in Queensland state schools demonstrates the conceptual significance of more localised studies of the type which have often occurred in the history of education space in Australia. It also demonstrates the importance of understanding secularisation as something changeable and place-dependent.

TABLE 6   Key moments in the banning of MACOS and SEMP

Date	Event
1973	MACOS trial began in selected Queensland primary schools.
1976	Queensland's contribution to the SEMP project was produced.
1977	Department of Education provided MACOS materials to additional schools for a wider trial.
17 January 1978	Cabinet banned MACOS against the recommendation of the Minister for Education.
21 February 1978	Cabinet elected not to approve SEMP for use in Queensland schools.
1980	Recommendations of the Select Committee on Education were released, leading to much of the SEMP material being permitted in Queensland schools.

In this case, the expert knowledge of teachers and curriculum developers was pitted against the arguments of an influential evangelical Protestant campaigner. In the first two months of 1978, the Queensland Cabinet, led by Premier Joh Bjelke-Petersen, made two important decisions relating to socials studies teaching in state schools. The first was to prohibit *Man: A Course of Study* (MACOS), a social studies program imported from America and used in primary schools. The second was to ban the *Social Education Materials Project* (SEMP), a diverse collection of materials created by groups from throughout Australia, including Queensland, and designed to be used across a range of secondary school subjects. These decisions were controversial, stirring public debate that played out across the pages of the state's daily newspaper and other media and drawing into focus the relationship between the Premier, and a prominent fundamentalist Christian morality campaigner, Rona Joyner. They also sparked a major inquiry into Queensland education. At the heart of these events lies a conflict between fundamentalist Christian and secular understandings of the role of the school in society.

The vetoing of the MACOS and SEMP materials cannot be understood without understanding the Premier leading the state at the time. Joh Bjelke-Petersen was such a controversial and divisive figure that, when one biographer sought to interview his former news and information officer for her book on the former Premier, she was asked whether she was writing "Jackboots Bjelke" or "Saint Joh."[194] Joh Bjelke-Petersen was Premier of Queensland from 1968–1987. Bjelke-Petersen, a member of the Country Party, which would become the National Party, was known for his conservative iteration of Lutheran Christianity, and for the personal mark he would place upon the state. The son of a Danish Lutheran pastor, Bjelke-Petersen was brought up between two wars as an adherent of a religion that was still largely associated with the enemy. Harrison notes that anti-German hysteria would likely have been felt by Danish Lutherans, due to the close association between this faith and Germany.[195] The debates around German schools, detailed in Part 2, and the use in these debates of the Lutheran faith as a proxy for a political ideology, nationalistic urges, and a belief in the continuation of language, would have had a direct impact on the Premier's family of origin. His public pronouncements reveal a belief that the church – here understood as that segment of Christian churches which adhere to his specific moral code – ought to retain a moral authority over the work of the state in education. During Bjelke-Petersen's period of governance, Queensland experienced controversies relating to sex education and the teaching of evolution in schools.[196] The school was therefore a significant ideological battleground in Queensland from the late 1960s through to the late 1980s.

John Harrison describes the dominant religious culture of Queensland since separation, particularly in the South Burnett community where Bjelke-Petersen grew up and lived, as pietistic.[197] This influence is evident throughout his history as Premier. His government's actions concerning education are evidence of a desire to create a generation of future citizens whose attitudes, values, and beliefs would be in line with a nationalistic, pietistic ethos. Such a belief system was challenged by SEMP and MACOS, both of which encouraged children to think about ongoing social issues in light of their own values, and both

---

194 Rae Wear, *Johannes Bjelke-Petersen: The Lord's Premier* (St Lucia, Qld.: Portland, Or: University of Queensland Press; Distributed in the USA and Canada by International Specialized Book Services, 2002), xi.

195 John Harrison, 'Faith in the Sunshine State: Joh Bjelke-Petersen and the Religious Culture of Queensland' (Doctor of Philosophy, St Lucia, University of Queensland, 1991), 55.

196 Katrina Barben, 'The Great Sex Education Pamphlet Scandal of 1971', *Queensland Journal of Labour History* 8 (2009): 19–23; John Wanna and Tracey Arklay, '12. The Government's Legislative Program, 1968–1989', in *The Ayes Have It: The History of the Queensland Parliament, 1957–1989* (Acton, ACT: ANU E Press, 2010), 425–67.

197 Harrison, 'Faith in the Sunshine State: Joh Bjelke-Petersen and the Religious Culture of Queensland'.

of which introduced children to the idea that people lived in ways other than those prescribed by mainstream Christianity.

Despite this influence, the Queensland population, in line with the Australian population as a whole, was becoming less overwhelmingly Christian. The 1976 Census showed that 78.6% of Australians identified as Christian. The percentage of Australians identifying as having no religion rose from 0.8% to 8.3% between 1966 and 1976.[198] Queensland was slightly more Christian and more religious overall than the national average, with 79.8% of Queenslanders adhering to some form of Christianity and 7.6% stating that they had no religion. By the end of Bjelke-Petersen's period of governance, 75.5% of Queenslanders were Christian while 11.7% had no religion.[199]

MACOS was introduced to Queensland primary schools in 1973. It was initially trialled in Geebung and Craigslea Primary Schools and Bamaga State High School. The results of this first trial suggested that MACOS could be a suitable addition to the social studies curriculum. Teachers from additional schools were offered training in the use of the program, during Christmas vacation summer schools, offered by the Department of Education.[200] In 1977, after it had been in use for four years, predominantly with children in grade six (10–11 years old), the Department of Education elected to provide four classroom sets of MACOS materials to each regional office in the state to allow a more extensive trial.[201] A report on teacher experiences using MACOS during that year indicated that teachers found the course fruitful and beneficial to their pupils. The same report indicated that due, in part, to criticisms of the program in the United States, it was important to communicate with parents and engage with criticisms of the program.[202] Seventeen Queensland primary schools began a trial of the program.[203] As Smith and Knight write, public debate over MACOS was spurred on by the visit of "textbook watcher" Mrs Mel Gabler, a Christian activist who had been instrumental in an American debate over the program. Gabler was a guest of Brisbane-based groups Society to Outlaw Pornography (STOP), with its adjunct group Committee Against Regressive

---

198   Australian Bureau of Statistics, 'Chapter – Religious Affiliation'.

199   'Chapter 3, Demography, Section 4', in *Queensland Past and Present: 100 Years of Statistics, 1896–1996* (Brisbane: Queensland Government, 2009), 88.

200   VJ Bird, 'For Cabinet RE: The Future Use of Man: A Course of Study (MACOS) in Queensland Schools', 1978, 2, Queensland State Archives.

201   KF Smith, *Man: A Course of Study. Its Use in Queensland Schools* (Queensland: Curriculum Branch, Department of Education, 1977), 3.

202   Ibid., 5.

203   'State Drops Course for Schools', *The Courier Mail*, 20 January 1978, 1, State Library of Queensland.

SECULARISATION IN AUSTRALIAN EDUCATION SINCE 1910   61

Education (CARE), and the Festival of Light, another fundamentalist group.[204] As Crowe, whose PhD dissertation examined STOP and CARE discovered, the membership of these groups was largely interchangeable.[205] Rona Joyner, the leader of STOP and CARE, would be a primary public figure in the banning of both MACOS and SEMP. Shirlee Robinson, in her account of homophobia in Queensland during Bjelke-Petersen's period of governance, notes that Joyner was particularly successful during this time due to Bjelke-Petersen's receptive attitude to her groups which, Robinson notes, "were particularly regressive about sexual matters."[206]

On January 17, 1978, the Queensland Cabinet decided to ban the MACOS program. It considered, in making this decision, a submission by the Minister for Education, VJ Bird. This submission noted that MACOS had received significant criticism during the latter part of 1977. The criticism considered by Bird was associated mainly with Rona Joyner herself. In considering this criticism, the Minister had taken into account views from members of the Parliamentary Education Committee, teachers, and members of Parents and Citizens' Associations of schools using the program. Finally, he sought advice from other Australian Ministers for Education.[207] Bird noted that no opposition to the program had been voiced in schools in which it had been trialled.[208] The negative reaction which had emerged, he wrote, had been led by STOP and CARE. He added that "[t]hese bodies are in fact a single organisation" and summarised the major criticisms made by the groups:

(a) The real aim of the course is to change the values of children, and to encourage them to accept values at variance with those generally held in our society;

(b) The course denigrates Christianity, teaches the theory of evolution, and advocates, among other things, violence, cannibalism, and polygamy; and

---

204   RA Smith and J Knight, 'MACOS in Queensland: The Politics of Educational Knowledge', *The Australian Journal of Education* 22, no. 3 (October 1978): 228.

205   Philip Henry Crowe, 'A Study of a Social Movement: The Dynamics of an Anti-Pornography Campaign in Queensland, Australia' (Doctor of Philosophy, Albany, State University of New York at Albany, 1976).

206   Shirleene Robinson, 'Homophobia as Party Politics: The Construction of the "homosexual Deviant" in Joh Bjelke-Petersen's Queensland', *Queensland Review* 17, no. 1 (2010): 32.

207   Bird, 'For Cabinet RE: The Future Use of Man: A Course of Study (MACOS) in Queensland Schools', 1.

208   Ibid., 3.

(c) The course is an American 'discard', which was offered in Australia only after its failure to achieve widespread acceptance in the United States.[209]

These objections, Bird wrote, could not be sustained. "In many cases," he wrote, "the charges are inaccurate and misleading and appear to be based on emotional rather than factual grounds."[210] This was particularly true, he indicated, of criticisms which held that the course denigrates Christianity or advocates violence.[211] Bird recommended that schools wishing to use MACOS be permitted to do so as long as any new schools wishing to employ the program provided adequate teacher training and sought parental permission.[212] This submission, which was made privately to Cabinet, and thus was not available to the public, had little impact. On January 19, 1978, Joh Bjelke-Petersen's cabinet announced a decision to ban MACOS from use in Queensland state schools.

On 7 February 1978, Cabinet asked the Minister for Education to present to Cabinet a submission explaining SEMP.[213] The document was provided ten days later. In this, the Minister included the report of a review committee that had examined the SEMP materials. Bird suggested that this report be provided to state secondary schools.[214] The majority of the SEMP materials were deemed either completely appropriate for all schools or appropriate with specific alterations and deletions.[215] On February 21, Cabinet decided not to approve SEMP for use in Queensland schools.[216]

The decision to ban MACOS and SEMP against the advice of the Minister for Education is attributable to the Premier of Queensland at the time, Joh Bjelke-Petersen. Bjelke-Petersen's pietistic views made him unusually sympathetic to the campaigns of Rona Joyner's STOP and CARE initiatives. To

---

209   Ibid., 4.

210   Ibid.

211   Ibid.

212   Bird, 'For Cabinet RE: The Future Use of Man: A Course of Study (MACOS) in Queensland Schools'.

213   Joh Bjelke-Petersen, 'Confidential Cabinet Minute. Decision No. 27761: Social Education Materials Project' (Queensland Government, 7 February 1978).

214   VJ Bird, 'For Cabinet. RE: Social Education Materials Project (SEMP)' (Queensland Government, 17 February 1978).

215   VJ Bird, 'For Cabinet. RE: Social Education Materials Project (SEMP). Appendix A: Summary of Recommendations on Materials Reviewed' (Queensland Government, 17 February 1978).

216   Bjelke-Petersen, 'Confidential Cabinet Minute. Decision No. 27761: Social Education Materials Project'.

SECULARISATION IN AUSTRALIAN EDUCATION SINCE 1910

refer to STOP and CARE as two groups is to overstate the point: the groups shared a newsletter, statements on their behalf were made conjointly, and they worked from the same headquarters. The foreword to a 1979 monograph refers to the groups jointly as "the group," and notes that it "is very largely one woman, Mrs Rona Joyner."[217] Joyner's political power existed only because the Bjelke-Petersen government was sympathetic to her concerns. Hers was not an uncontroversial or generally accepted viewpoint. It was, however, a viewpoint that was solicited for inclusion in various media reports and which was seen to influence the Queensland government.

An outspoken conservative Christian, Joyner was a noted public figure concerned with issues relating to morality and, particularly, children and youth. She was the subject of much derision, and her influence in this debate is, on the face of it, extremely surprising. Her capacity to shape policy was dependent upon, and embedded within, the power structures in Queensland at the time. As such, her role in this case highlights the significance of Martin's observation that the power of religious groups is deeply associated with how local elites conceptualise history and society.[218] Scott and Scott note that that "[v]ery few educationalists or academic students of education would wish to be seen near Mrs Joyner and all she stands for."[219] Certainly, the beliefs she expressed about education at the time were out of line with prevailing views among teachers and academics.

Joyner's main line of argument was that children should not be taught anything which contradicted Christian teachings. This is exemplified in her submission to the Select Committee of Inquiry into Education in Queensland, which was formed partly in response to the public outcry over the banning of MACOS and SEMP. She told the committee that:

> Education must never be in conflict with the family; if it is, then it is not education, but value-changing and propaganda. SEMP breaks this fundamental rule! It creates the vehicle to drive the children away from their parents by introducing soft meaningless group concensus [sic.] subjects

---

217 Mayer in Ann Gowers and Roger Scott, *Fundamentals and Fundamentalists: A Case-Study of Education and Policy-Making in Queensland*, APSA Monograph, no. 22 (Bedford Park, S. Aust: Australasian Political Studies Association, 1979), iii.

218 Martin, 'Secularization', 465.

219 Ann Scott and Roger Scott, *Reform and Reaction in the Deep North: Education and Policy-Making in Queensland* (Parkville, Melbourne: Centre for the Study of Higher Education: University of Melbourne, 1980), iii.

of secular Humanism, and deprives children of the hard disciplines of real information absorption – in short, of their cultural heritage.[220]

Joyner believed that education must support traditional family structures and not challenge what she viewed as the cultural heritage of Australian children. For her, secular education, and specifically education which she saw as aligned with 'secular humanism,' was in direct conflict with Christianity.

Joyner further argued that social science education displaced traditional subjects and imbued children and young people with Marxist values. She described the aim of the social sciences as:

> to graduate illiterates in geography and history – to bring into being the Marxist concept of removing one generation of children from their heritage (family, nation and religion). For all purposes, history and geography have now disappeared from education![221]

This argument appealed to Cold War-era tensions between Marxism and capitalism as competing economic systems. It is also an argument that continues to be used by individuals and groups opposing progressive education reform.[222] Joyner further argued that the SEMP materials were based on a false assumption, this being that Australia is a "multi-cultural pluralist society," whereas, she argued, "in actual fact Australia is constituted a CHRISTIAN pluralist country [emphasis in original]."[223] Joyner furthered her argument by suggesting that parents, particularly parents from disadvantaged backgrounds, failed to teach their children Christian morality.

She stated that SEMP did not compensate "for any deficiency of Christian culture and moral social habit in the backgrounds of disadvantaged students," but instead encouraged "further disadvantaging of children by attempting to destroy and remove Christian influence altogether."[224] She argued that SEMP

---

220 Rona Joyner, 'SEMP: The Case against. Submission to the Select Committee of Inquiry into Education (QLD)', n.d., ii.

221 Ibid.

222 Rob Cover et al., 'Progress in Question: The Temporalities of Politics, Support and Belonging in Gender- and Sexually-Diverse Pedagogies', *Continuum*, 7 February 2017, 1–13, https://doi.org/10.1080/10304312.2017.1281883.

223 Joyner, 'SEMP: The Case against. Submission to the Select Committee of Inquiry into Education (QLD)', ii.

224 Ibid., 1.

SECULARISATION IN AUSTRALIAN EDUCATION SINCE 1910   65

condoned and encouraged "every form of 'alternative' lifestyle and anti-social behaviour."[225]

It is clear that, for Joyner, SEMP and MACOS represented a threat to what she perceived as the existing ordering of society. Indeed, she explicitly stated that the aim of "humanistic education" is to "change children's thinking and behaviour, in order that through children society might be changed."[226, 227] For Joyner, SEMP was particularly threatening because "SEMP is dealing with the things right here in our own society – not in a distant Eskimo society as in MACOS."[228] The "things" to which she objected included non-judgemental references to homosexuality, divorce, and unmarried parenthood. Joyner viewed the SEMP materials as "social engineering."[229]

While Joyner's arguments may otherwise have been on the fringe of public discourse, they occurred in a context in which the Queensland government was particularly receptive to claims rooted in conservative Christian morality. In public pronouncements, the Queensland Government took the position that it had the right to constrain immoral or inappropriate teaching. For example, on Thursday, February 23, 1978, *The Courier-Mail* announced that SEMP had been banned. The front page bore a telling statement by the Premier:

> JOH: There is someone in the Education Department who does not seem to know what the Government wants to be taught.[230]

Bjelke-Petersen was further quoted as having said that:

> Educators will get the message that we will only allow wholesome, decent practical material in schools.[231]

The materials used in schools were therefore positioned in relation to a moral hierarchy, wherein only materials which met the moral standards of the government could be employed. Government figures did not, however, explicitly refer to religious faith. Bjelke-Petersen's statement that "someone in the Education Department" did not know what the government wanted to be

---

225   Ibid.
226   Ibid., 2.
227   Ibid., 2.
228   'New Education Material Attacked', *The Courier Mail*, 2 February 1978, 9.
229   'Course Attacked', *The Courier Mail*, 16 February 1978, 17.
230   'School Study Aid Scrapped', *The Courier Mail*, 23 February 1978, 1.
231   Ibid.

taught, appears to imply that this moral hierarchy ought to have been known and understood by decision-makers. In this article, the Education Minister, Val Bird, was quoted as having denied that Joyner and CARE had any impact on the decision. It is clear from the Cabinet records that Bird himself had no impact on the decision – like MACOS, SEMP was banned from use in Queensland state schools against his recommendation. However, the government presented a unified front wherein it was responsible and able to make determinations on the subject of public morality.

The banning of MACOS and SEMP was a significant challenge to the autonomy and professionalism of teachers which has remained in the memory of Queensland teachers and serves as a cautionary tale. This is exemplified by a summary of the case published in the *Queensland Teachers' Journal* in 2006:

> In early 1978, the Queensland Coalition Cabinet, led by Premier Joh Bjelke-Petersen, banned from state schools two innovative educational resources: first MACOS (Man: A Course of Study) then SEMP (Social Education Materials Project). The bans were not in response to concerns held by teachers, parents, students, educational experts or anyone else with a connection to the state school system, but by born-again (from atheism) fundamental Christian Rona Joyner.[232]

Teachers highlighted their role as professionals and the instability of this role in a situation wherein curricula could be changed with little warning. This line of argument is demonstrated by the position of QTU president, Mr L Schuntner, articulated at a public meeting in opposition to the banning of MACOS:

> The job of teachers is becoming untenable if every week or two we are going to hear of some new intervention at the political level on what we are to teach or not to teach.[233]

A similar line of argument emerged from teachers, principals, and other educational professionals involved with non-government schools. The decision to ban MACOS and SEMP applied only to Queensland's state schools. Non-government schools were not bound by the decision of the Premier and

---

232 Nicole Mathieson, 'Remembering the Bad Old Days', *Queensland Teachers' Journal*, 23 November 2006, 6.

233 'Protest on Scrapping of MACOS', *The Courier Mail*, 25 January 1978, 3, State Library of Queensland.

SECULARISATION IN AUSTRALIAN EDUCATION SINCE 1910

Cabinet. Taking up the position that teachers are professionals and should be trusted to make sound educational judgements, the chairman of the Queensland Branch of the Headmasters' Conference of Independent Schools of Australia wrote to *The Courier-Mail* objecting to the decision to ban the material. He stated:

> Whilst the decision to make use of any or all of the material is one for each Independent School to make, and our right to use the material is not in question, our concern over the banning of all s.e.m.p. material is that the integrity and good judgement of many responsible educators in Australia have been called into question and the community of Queensland polarised on an issue before the majority of teachers and parents had had a chance to assess the material.[234]

Other educators, including Professor Evans of the University of Queensland, took the stance that public opposition to the MACOS and SEMP was based on misconceptions. Focusing on SEMP, he stated that the project had created resources concerned with "teaching young Australians about different aspects of modern society – geography, history, social studies, home economics, social science, English, art, commerce, economics, environmental studies, and science."[235] The purpose of SEMP materials, he indicated, was to provide relevant information about social issues in Australia and the world and, unlike textbooks, to encourage students to discuss and question these issues. This, he said, was a response to the difficulties of social education, wherein controversial topics should be taught in a balanced, thoughtful way. "These have been the concerns of SEMP," he wrote. "They are also the concerns of teachers, parents, and the community at large."[236] Here, SEMP is positioned as a reasonable response to a pluralistic society. The idea that Australian society is an inherently Christian society, which was significant in Joyner's arguments, was implicitly rejected by all of the educators opposed to the bans. Instead, they represented teachers as expert educators working to enable their students to be critical thinkers and responsible citizens in a diverse society. These perspectives, however, were implicitly rejected by the government.

---

234   MA Howell, 'Private Schools Hit SEMP Ban', *The Courier Mail*, 1 March 1978, Item ID 198873.

235   Glen Evans, 'SEMP: It's Designed to Help Students', *The Courier Mail*, 22 February 1978, 5.

236   Ibid.

A Case of Desecularisation?

This case highlights the significance of Eisenstadt's theory of multiple modernities to understanding secularisation.[237] The position of Christianity in Queensland's political culture during this period was unusual when compared with the rest of the Australian states. This was a time in which, as popular lore has it, visitors to Queensland from the southern states of Australia would joke that they had to set their watches back fifty years.[238] There was a conservative, deeply Christian, ideology associated with Bjelke-Petersen's government. Just as Spohn argued, neither secularisation nor modernisation is a useful master narrative.[239] There is no single trajectory of religious change. Thus, it is possible for a shift in Queensland state school curricula favouring a form of conservative Christianity to occur more or less contemporaneously with a shift in Federal Government policy, which highlights and recognises the non-religious function of religious non-government schools.

This case also emphasises the significant role that powerful figures and personalities can play in determining the outcomes of instances of potential secularisation. Possamai has suggested that the twenty-first century has seen religion become more prevalent and accepted in the public sphere.[240] However, this case demonstrates the extent to which a single political leader can, in themselves, alter the realm of the sayable, constituting a specific type of religion as a significant determinant and indicator of public morality. This highlights a moment during which a religious campaigner effected a backlash against perceived secularisation and a reassertion of the right of Christians to have their morality determine what is taught to the next generation. The fact that MACOS and SEMP were banned demonstrates the power of the Premier of Queensland at this time, and the decision of the Queensland population to continue electing someone who was known for his conservative religious values. All of this suggests that this was a moment during which Christianity reclaimed its power over some aspects of social studies curriculum content.

Conclusion

The tensions of the 1960s and 1970s, as they emerged in Australia, resonate with international concerns and areas of contention. The banning of MACOS,

---

237 Eisenstadt, 'Multiple Modernities'.

238 E.g. Shakira Hussein, 'Frozen in Time: Sharing a Queensland Childhood with David Malouf', The Wheeler Centre, 14 April 2014, http://www.wheelercentre.com/notes/b4095 b8db24c.

239 Spohn, 'Multiple Modernity, Nationalism and Religion'.

240 Possamai, *Religion and Popular Culture*, 33.

in particular, can be understood in association with the actions of the Christian right in the United States. However, as these cases demonstrate, even within a single country, secularisation does not occur at the same rate and instances of churches or Christian groups being given increased control can happen for very different reasons. These cases also demonstrate the significance of the personality of individual leaders in determining the outcome of claims made by dominant faith groups. This theme is again highlighted in the next part, which examines a series of twenty-first-century debates.

Part 4: Twenty-First Century Debates: Christian Influence in a Complex System

Introduction

This part focuses on the place of Christianity in contemporary Australian state-run primary and secondary education. In a context of increased religious diversity, and an increasing proportion of Australians claiming a non-religious identity, the presumption that state education systems will be "secular" has been strengthened. It is no longer easy, or realistic, to claim that Australia is a Christian nation or to appeal to shared Protestant values. Despite this, Christian beliefs continue to be influential in debates over curricula, and primarily Christian programs of religious instruction and chaplaincy continue to be supported in state schools.[241] This part examines two case studies that highlight both the extent and the limits of what might be described as Christian incursions into secular state schooling. The first case study focuses on two challenges to government-funded chaplaincy, while the second examines the simultaneous introduction of an LGBTIQ program and review of religious instruction materials in Queensland.

Secular Systems? Religion in Contemporary Australian Education

One key space in which Christianity and education intersect in the Australian system is in religious education and religious instruction. As Parker identifies in the first volume of this series, *Religion and Education, Framing and Mapping a Field*, debates about religious education often fail to recognise that the term

---

241 Maddox, *Taking God to School*; Byrne, *Religion in Secular Education*; Carden, "'Fiddling with Young Kiddies' Minds'".

has multiple meanings.[242] Religious Instruction, in the Australian context, is akin to what Parker describes as "religious education as practical theology."[243] This form of instruction is presented in domination-specific environments, even where it takes place in public schools, and involves teaching the tenets of faith in a way that is intended to apply to the social environment in which young people live. Religious education refers more to ideas of what Parker defines as "religious education as religious literacy" and "religious education as intercultural/interreligious education," a process that allows for the development of the knowledge and understanding of religion required for citizenship in a diverse society.[244]

Goldburg examined the shifting religious curriculum in Australian schools from the 1980s. She explains that a faith-forming approach, centred on religious instruction, was the primary means through which religion entered schools before this period. Since then, however, some schools have begun offering comparative studies in religion. In Queensland, this course is not offered in state schools but is offered as an alternative to traditional religious instruction in many non-government, faith-based schools.[245]

Byrne argues that secular religion and ethics courses provide an appropriate alternative to religious instruction. She states that "[c]hildren have an internationally recognised human right to understand religion." To understand this, she states, they must be aware of how religion works on "human motivation, inspiration and ethical deliberation."[246] A secular religion and ethics course, she argues, would allow for dialogue between religious and non-religious views, and teach children to be open, respectful, and critical of alternative perspectives. Despite this, Byrne notes that there are significant impediments to the ongoing development of secular studies of religion courses. These impediments include the fact that no Australian university currently offers studies in religion as a pedagogical focus area for student-teachers, and the fact that a growing number of accredited teacher training colleges are operated by Christian, often Evangelical Pentecostal groups.

---

242   Stephen G Parker, 'Religion and Education: Framing and Mapping a Field', in *Religion and Education: Framing and Mapping a Field*, ed. Stephen G Parker et al., Brill Research Perspectives in Religion and Education, 2019, 12.

243   Ibid., 13.

244   Ibid., 14.

245   Peta Goldburg, 'Teaching Religion in Australian Schools', *Numen* 55, no. 2 (1 April 2008): 261, https://doi.org/10.1163/156852708X283069.

246   Byrne, *Religion in Secular Education*, 267.

SECULARISATION IN AUSTRALIAN EDUCATION SINCE 1910

Another key pathway through which primarily Christian religion enters Australian "secular" state schools in the twenty-first century is through school chaplaincy. Chaplaincy has an extensive history in Australian schools. For example, Judith Salecich writes that there is evidence that unpaid chaplains worked in some Queensland state secondary schools during the 1970s and 1980s, with the first paid chaplain appointed to a Queensland school in 1987, while the first chaplain trained and appointed by Scripture Union Queensland (SUQ), which remains the primary provider of chaplains today, was appointed in 1990.[247] By the mid-1990s, chaplains were an accepted part of Australian schools, predominantly secondary schools, but chaplaincy was not funded by state or federal governments. In October 2006, the then-Prime Minister of Australia, John Howard, announced the National School Chaplaincy Program (NSCP). The program provided funds to allow schools to hire paid chaplains, who were required to be recognised members of a religious group.[248] It was voluntary and involved both private and public schools. While the program was explicitly religious, it was not explicitly Christian. The funding meant that chaplains, who had previously worked almost exclusively in secondary schools, began to be present in growing numbers of primary schools.

If schools chose to participate in the NSCP, they were not permitted to select a non-religious chaplain. They were, however, allowed to select the religious affiliation of their chaplain. From 2012–2014 secular welfare workers could also be funded under the program. This was, however, a short-lived change, made by a Labor government and scrapped when the Liberal Party returned to power. From the outset, and at the time of writing, only religious chaplains are funded. It is not a requirement that they are Christian. However, in 2012, of the 2607 chaplains funded in Australia, 2593 (99.5%) were Christian.[249] Chaplaincy is, therefore, in practice, an overwhelmingly Christian endeavour. This is despite the fact that chaplains are not permitted to proselytise or discuss religion unless they are explicitly asked to do so by students. At the same time, chaplains are not permitted to provide religious instruction during their working hours. They may do so in a volunteer capacity, outside of their paid work time. Their role is primarily related to pastoral care through being a contact point for students who need to talk and through organising events. They

---

247 Judith Anne Salecich, 'Chaplaincy in Queensland State Schools: An Investigation' (Doctor of Philosophy, St Lucia, University of Queensland, 2002), 1, https://espace.library.uq.edu.au/view/UQ:184700.

248 John Howard, 'Media Release: National School Chaplaincy Program', 29 October 2006.

249 Jeremy Patrick, 'Religion, Secularism, and the National School Chaplaincy and Student Welfare Program', *University of Queensland Law Journal* 33, no. 1 (2014): 205.

also take on other roles within the school, such as monitoring student behaviour in playgrounds or other spaces during lunch breaks. They are therefore in the position of serving as a (usually) Christian presence within the school without, in the majority of their work, performing any uniquely Christian function. In Case Study 5, I examine two successful legal challenges to school chaplaincy in the High Court of Australia, identifying the justifications for the federal government manoeuvres which permitted the continuation of the programme even after it had been ruled unconstitutional.

Case Study 5: Challenges to School Chaplaincy

In 2012, and again in 2014, a Queensland parent, Ron Williams, successfully challenged Federal Government funding for school chaplaincy in the High Court of Australia. It is perhaps unsurprising that these challenges originated from Queensland. The state's uptake of the program was particularly high. As a result of the NSCP, between 2006 and 2010, the number of chaplains in Queensland state schools had grown from 200 to 600.[250] In 2011, one-third of all Australian government schools accessing chaplains were in Queensland.[251] Despite the success of these challenges, subsequent federal governments continued to support chaplaincy and to reinvigorate models of funding it. Their justifications, and the arguments of those opposing chaplaincy programs, provide important insight into the relationship between what might be understood as Christian and secular concepts in twenty-first-century Australian educational policy.

Williams' first challenge reached the High Court of Australia on August 9, 2011. He challenged the Darling Heights Funding Agreement, under which chaplaincy at his children's school was funded. The defendants in the case were the Commonwealth of Australia, the Commonwealth Minister for School Education, Early Childhood and Youth, the Commonwealth Minister for Finance and Deregulation, and SUQ. Williams argued that the funding was invalid because it was:

a) beyond the executive power of the Commonwealth under s61 of the Constitution
b) prohibited by s 116 of the Constitution.[252]

---

250   David John Pohlmann, 'School Chaplaincy in Queensland State Schools: A Case Study' (Doctor of Philosophy, Brisbane, Logan, Griffith University, 2010), 4.

251   Marilyn Harrington, 'School Chaplains', Parliament of Australia: Flagpost, 15 July 2011, https://www.aph.gov.au/About_Parliament/Parliamentary_Departments/Parliamentary _Library/FlagPost/2011/July/School_chaplains.

252   CJ French, J Hayne, J Crennan, J Kiefel, J Bell, J Gummow, et al., Williams v Commonwealth of Australia & Ors., No. HCA 23 (High Court of Australia 20 June 2012).

SECULARISATION IN AUSTRALIAN EDUCATION SINCE 1910 73

TABLE 7   Major events in Australian school chaplaincy, 2011–2015

Date	Event
9 August 2011	First challenge reached High Court.
8 September 2011	Minister for Education, Peter Garrett, announces changes to NSCP. From 2012 program would be known as the National School Chaplaincy and Student Welfare Program. The chaplaincy budget was expanded, and secular welfare workers could also be funded.
20 June 2012	First High Court decision handed down. The NSCP was declared unconstitutional because it was not funded under any legislation.
28 June 2012	The *Financial Framework Legislation Amendment Act (No. 3) (2012)* was assented to, allowing funding for chaplaincy to continue.
6 May 2014	Second challenge reached High Court.
13 May 2014	2014 Federal budget removes funding for secular welfare workers. Only religious chaplains are to be funded under the NSCP.
19 June 2014	High Court overturns funding for chaplaincy on the basis that the relevant provisions of the *Financial Framework Legislation Amendment Act (No. 3) (2012)* were not supported by any legislative head of power under the Constitution.
From 2015	Federal funding for chaplaincy granted to state and territory governments rather than directly to schools.

During the ongoing challenge, the then Federal Minister for School Education, Peter Garrett, announced changes to the National School Chaplaincy Program, including the provision that secular welfare workers could be funded by the chaplaincy programme. Garrett himself is known for his deeply-held Christian faith.[253] Minimum qualifications for chaplains were also introduced. A post on the website of the Australian Parliament stated that "[i]t will be interesting to see how those involved in the High Court challenge to the NSCP, which still looms over the program's future, will respond" to the changes.[254] One group

---

253   Peter Garrett, Peter Garrett: 'Kevin Rudd betrayed the faith', interview by Andrew West, Radio, 11 November 2015, http://www.abc.net.au/radionational/programs/religion andethicsreport/peter-garrett-kevin-rudd-betrayed-the-faith-labor-christianity/6931250.

254   Marilyn Harrington, 'Changes to the National School Chaplaincy Program', Parliament of Australia, 9 August 2011, http://www.aph.gov.au/About_Parliament/Parliamentary

which did respond was the Australian Christian Lobby (ACL), which released a media statement demanding that funding for secular welfare workers be provided by a different program, not from the same funding pool as chaplains.[255] The then-Shadow Minister for Education, Christopher Pyne, said that:

> The secularists who are taking the Chaplains to the High Court will chalk this up as a first victory in the campaign to dismantle the Chaplaincy programme.[256]

The use of 'secularists' as an identifier or naming practice suggests a binary between supporters of chaplaincy, and a group seeking a radically secular change. The High Court's decision was handed down in 2012. The Court agreed that the funding was beyond the executive power of the Commonwealth. It did not, however, agree that it was prohibited by s116 of the Constitution, which reads that:

> The Commonwealth shall not make any law for establishing any religion, or for imposing any religious observance, or for prohibiting the free exercise of any religion, and no religious test shall be required as a qualification for any office or public trust under the Commonwealth.[257]

This argument was quickly dismissed on the basis that, while religion could not be a requirement for officeholders under the Commonwealth of Australia, chaplains employed by SUQ did not hold office under the Commonwealth, nor engage in any contract with the Commonwealth.[258] Legal scholar Beck criticises the limited guidance offered by the High Court on the religious test clause of the Australian Constitution.[259] The outcome was mixed. The funding

---

_Departments/Parliamentary_Library/FlagPost/2011/September/Changes_to_the _National_School_Chaplaincy_Program.

255 Australian Christian Lobby, 'Media Release: Govt Must Find New Money for Secular School Workers, Not Dilute Chaplaincy Money', 7 September 2011.

256 Christopher Pyne, 'Media Release: Gillard Backhands Rudd over Chaplains', 7 September 2011.

257 Parliament of Australia, 'Commonwealth of Australia Constitution Act', § s. 127 (1901), sec. 116, http://www.aph.gov.au/About_Parliament/Senate/Powers_practice_n_procedures/~/link.aspx?_id=AFF6CA564BC3465AA325E73053DED4AA&_z=z#chapter-01_part-05_51.

258 French, Hayne, Crennan, Kiefel, Bell, Gummow, et al., Williams v Commonwealth of Australia & Ors.

259 Luke Beck, 'Williams v Commonwealth: School Chaplains and the Religious Tests Clause of the Constitution', *Monash Law Review* 38, no. 3 (2012): 271–94.

SECULARISATION IN AUSTRALIAN EDUCATION SINCE 1910

arrangements were invalidated. In this sense, Williams was successful in his challenge. The question of the separation of church and state, however, was not answered in his favour. The invalidation of the funding arrangements was made on the basis that there was no statutory authority for the funding. The decision left the door open for alternative funding arrangements to be constructed using new legislation.

Federal Attorney-General, Nicola Roxon, and Federal Minister for Education, Peter Garrett held a media conference immediately after the High Court of Australia decision in 2012 and reassured the public that the chaplaincy program would continue. The decision had a broad impact, one that went beyond funding for chaplaincy. Cheryl Saunders, Professor of Law at Melbourne University, told Radio National's *Law Report* that:

> The reason for the panic is that there were so many Commonwealth executive schemes without supporting legislation that were potentially called into question by this decision of the court.[260]

The program stated that the decision impacted around ten percent of government expenditure. The Commonwealth Government responded by passing the *Financial Framework Legislation Amendment Act (No. 3)* (2012). According to the constitutional lawyer Anne Twomey, the Act gave the Executive the power to spend money without parliamentary scrutiny or legislation.[261] This had the effect of rectifying the immediate effects of the outcomes of the Williams case but left open the door for another challenge.

The second High Court challenge began on 6 May 2014. SUQ was again a respondent in the case, joined by the Commonwealth of Australia and the Minister for Education.[262] Williams argued successfully that the legislation providing for the chaplaincy funding was unlawful, and that the funding of chaplaincy was beyond the executive power of the Commonwealth.[263]

---

260 'Challenge to School Chaplaincy Program Gearing up for High Court', *Law Report* (Australian Broadcasting Commission Radio National, 7 August 2012), http://www .abc.net.au/radionational/programs/lawreport/chaplaincy-high-court-challenge-232/ 4180562#transcript.

261 Anne Twomey, 'Bringing down the House? Keeping School Chaplains Means a Surrender to the Executive', The Conversation, 27 June 2012, http://theconversation.com/bringing -down-the-house-keeping-school-chaplains-means-a-surrender-to-the-executive-7926.

262 'Transcript: Williams v Commonwealth of Australia & Ors [2014] HCATrans 92' (High Court of Australia, 6 May 2014).

263 CJ French, J Hayne, J Crennan, J Kiefel, J Bell, and J Keane, Williams v Commonwealth of Australia & Ors., No. HCA 23 (High Court of Australia 19 June 2014).

The respondents argued that funding for chaplaincy constituted providing benefits for students. This argument held that such funding was within the Commonwealth's powers under the Constitution, which allows:

> the provision of maternity allowances, widows' pensions, child endowment, unemployment, pharmaceutical, sickness and hospital benefits, medical and dental services (but not so as to authorise any form of civil conscription), benefits to students and family allowances.[264]

In its ruling of 19 June 2014, the Court found that the provisions allowing for school chaplaincy did not meet the definition listed above.[265] Nor were other legal arguments for the continuation of chaplaincy considered valid. The "benefits" provided by the chaplaincy program were not "benefits" of a sort intended to provide for the material needs of any identified or identifiable student, and they were not directed toward the consequences of being a student.[266]

The judgement included statements that may be interpreted as supporting the chaplaincy program, such as the following:

> For the purposes of argument, it may be accepted that some students would derive advantage from using the services and, in that sense, *should* do so. But no student and no member of the school community *must* do so. All may; perhaps some should; none must.[267]

"Perhaps some should" is mild language. However, the judgement also included this more explicitly positive statement:

> [T]he only description of how the "support" is to be given is that it includes "strengthening values, providing pastoral care and enhancing engagement with the broader community". These are desirable ends.[268]

The judgement did not interpret the meaning of values, pastoral care, or engagement in this context. These terms are left unremarked upon, as though they have a common-sense definition. This is despite the fact that 'pastoral

---

264 Parliament of Australia, Commonwealth of Australia Constitution Act, sec. 41xxiiiA.
265 French, Hayne, Crennan, Kiefel, Bell, and Keane, Williams v Commonwealth of Australia & Ors.
266 Ibid., para. 47.
267 Ibid., para. 42.
268 Ibid., para. 47.

care,' in particular, is a term with historical links to Christian practice.[269] SUQ was quick to respond to the ruling, stating that the Court had made a decision about the balance between State and Federal Government powers, and had not delivered "an anti-chaplaincy ruling."[270]

SUQ's Peter James highlighted the favourable comments the Court made about school chaplaincy.[271] He said that the funding arrangements had been found unconstitutional because chaplaincy "benefits" all students. James also called for an alternative funding solution and said that: "[i]n my own state, in Queensland, I know that the state is very supportive of the program."[272] This case, like the first, had wider ramifications. The Court's 2014 decision invalidated the funding arrangements for 427 government programs, in addition to the chaplaincy program.[273] Chaplaincy providers had sufficient funding to last until the end of 2015. Before this time, a new scheme was implemented by the Commonwealth Government, which allowed for the continuation of the program through grants to the states.

Australian Prime Ministers, since Howard, have supported chaplaincy, drawing on the argument that chaplains provided valuable support for students beyond, and regardless of, any religious function. In introducing government-funded chaplaincy, the then-Prime Minister, John Howard, initially described the role of chaplains in broad terms, stating that "chaplains will be expected to provide pastoral care, general religious and personal advice and comfort and support to students and staff, irrespective of their religious beliefs."[274] His description of the function of chaplains included roles that are not religious. This emphasis on the non-religious function of chaplains resonates with the findings of Maddox's work on religiosity in the Howard era, which showed that Howard, and members of his government, were experts at appealing to the idea of Christianity without making explicit theological references.[275]

One of the most interesting factors, in this case, is the support for chaplaincy of Prime Ministers Julia Gillard and Tony Abbott. An atheist, and a devout

---

269   Carmen Schuhmann and Annelieke Damen, 'Representing the Good: Pastoral Care in a Secular Age', *Pastoral Psychology* 67, no. 4 (August 2018): 405–17, https://doi.org/10.1007/s11089-018-0826-0.

270   Scripture Union Queensland, 'The High Court's Decision Is In ...', *SU QLD Back Our Chappies* (blog), 2014, https://www.suqld.org.au/highcourt.

271   Ibid.

272   Ibid.

273   Lauren Wilson and Jennifer Rajca, 'Unholy Mess', *The Courier Mail*, 20 June 2014, 6.

274   Howard, 'Media Release: National School Chaplaincy Program'.

275   Maddox, *God under Howard*.

Catholic respectively, both were members of groups that have traditionally been opposed to religious teaching in state schools. Catholics were among the groups most vehemently opposed to the introduction of religious instruction into Queensland's state schools, as highlighted in Part 2, while declared atheists were not numerous enough to operate as a separate and meaningful political unit. However, as Bouma has shown, the sectarian conflicts between Catholics and Protestants became less politically significant as Australia became more religiously diverse during the latter part of the twentieth century.[276] This does not suggest that sectarianism necessarily disappeared, merely that religious differences have been remapped within the context of new religious diversities. Tony Abbott's support of school chaplaincy may be understood in light of a new political allegiance formed between these two groups of Christians. Indeed, Scripture Union, including SUQ, uses the term 'Christian' rather than 'Protestant' to denote their religious affiliation, obscuring traditional splits between Protestant and Catholic believers.[277] Gillard's support, however, was justified in light of the purported secular benefits of school chaplaincy. When the first case was pending in 2011, Gillard stated that:

> The school chaplaincy scheme is a great scheme and because we think it's such a good scheme we promised at the election last year to extend it. I've had the opportunity to meet a lot of chaplains and go to a lot of schools and get the feedback that school chaplains provide that extra bit of pastoral care which can often make a real difference in a child's life.[278]

Pastoral care is here portrayed as something that can make a positive difference in the life of a child. It is not, however, defined. The concept of pastoral care remains a nebulous one. It has not been clearly articulated by actors on either side of the debate. As noted above, the term was used in the High Court judgement's second case as a description of a good which could be offered to all students. The word, however, is a Christian religious term. It is also something that has been positioned as different from, but similar to, counselling. For example, when Tony Abbott spoke to radio host Ray Hadley about the new arrangements for funding after the second High Court challenge, he

---

276 Gary D Bouma, 'Social Justice Issues in the Management of Religious Diversity in Australia', *Social Justice Research* 12, no. 4 (1999).

277 Scripture Union, 'Scripture Union, Australia', 2018, http://scriptureunion.org.au/.

278 Julia Gillard, 'Transcript of Joint Doorstop Interview, Sydney' (PM Transcripts, 1 January 2011), https://pmtranscripts.pmc.gov.au/release/transcript-17561.

emphasised that the only acceptable plan would be one in which the states were not permitted to fund non-religious workers. He stated that "we want to ensure that this money really does produce chaplaincy services because there are already a range of counselling services in schools, and this is not just for general counselling, this is for chaplaincy."[279]

Secular, but Religious?

This case, and the justifications offered for the continuation of school chaplaincy, highlight the ongoing awkward position of chaplains in Australian schools. They must act as a religious presence in schools, but cannot proselytise. Their role demonstrates both the extent and limits of the privilege available to Christian faith groups in Australian state schools. It is possible to have a government-funded role in state schools that is only open to a person of faith. In the vast majority of cases, this person of faith is a Christian. At the same time, proselytising is not permitted. The resulting situation is one in which Christian faith can be a mandatory requirement for a position in a public school, but the person holding that position is unable to express that faith except in specific, relatively constrained, circumstances.

The arguments over school chaplaincy bring to light the apparent function of the Christian religion outside of, and above, promoting and supporting a belief in the supernatural. While school chaplains could ostensibly be of any faith, the reality of the situation is that the overwhelming majority of chaplains were, and are, Christian. Key theorists in the 1960s and 1970s secularisation movement demonstrated that religion has important social functions in terms of providing justifications for institutions and providing symbols of solemnity.[280] The arguments of supporters of school chaplaincy reveal another critical contemporary symbolic function of Christianity. That a person whose primary qualification is adhering to the Christian faith should be seen as an appropriate support person for young people, including young people going through crises, speaks to the ongoing symbolic value of Christianity, as a marker of goodness or trustworthiness. Just as Maddox has shown that Australians view (Christian) religion as a "good thing for political leaders to have,"[281] the proponents of school chaplaincy appear to view this faith as a positive trait for school employees to have. Despite this continuing symbolic

---

279 Tony Abbott, Interview with Ray Hadley, Radio 2GB, Sydney, interview by Ray Hadley, Transcript of radio broadcast, 20 June 2014, https://pmtranscripts.pmc.gov.au/release/transcript-23585.

280 Berger, *The Social Reality of Religion*, 42; Wilson, *Religion in Secular Society: A Sociological Comment*, 18.

281 Maddox, *God under Howard*, 142.

function of Christianity, these debates have demonstrated that there is a willingness, on the part of both supporters and opponents of school chaplaincy, to position state schools as secular spaces. What this means, however, is contested. While opponents of school chaplaincy appear to accept a secular/religious binary, supporters adopt something more akin to Crockett's idea of secular spaces as locations in which religion may be discussed, albeit under controlled circumstances.[282]

For some proponents of chaplaincy, the fact that schools are a secular space appears to be a factor that renders chaplains necessary: they can provide a Christian role model and spiritual guidance to students who may otherwise struggle to live out their faith in such an environment. While few would contest the point that institutional Christian religion has less cultural power in the twenty-first century than it did in the past, this does not negate the continuing significance of religion in individual lives.[283] The presence of chaplaincy in schools serves to affirm that Christianity, as a historically dominant religion, continues to have a privileged place in Australia.

A significant factor ensuring the continued operation of school chaplaincy has been the ability of chaplaincy providers, including SUQ, to assert the value of their service outside of religious terms. In the context of the multi-scalar, multi-faceted definition of secularisation proposed in Part 1, it is possible to understand the decision of para-church groups to take on non-religious roles through the lens of Dobbelaere's concept of organisational secularisation. From this perspective, churches or related groups retain relevance in a secularised society by offering non-religious services and articulating a more extensive social purpose.[284]

Interestingly, legal scholars have weighed in on the extent to which chaplaincy represents a threat to the idea of a secular state. Ahdar argues that they pose no such threat.[285] For him, chaplains fulfil a non-religious function. Patrick agrees that chaplains carry out a role that is almost entirely secular. However, he notes that, while it is in theory, religiously neutral, chaplaincy in Australia is, in fact, an overwhelmingly Christian endeavour.[286] He indicates that a program that employs workers based on their religious faith but

---

282 Clayton Crockett, 'Post-Secularism, Secular Theology, and the Names of the Real', *Dialog* 54, no. 4 (2015): 317–26.

283 Possamai, *Religion and Popular Culture*, 32.

284 Dobbelaere, *Secularization*, 113.

285 Rex Tauati Ahdar, 'A Real Threat or a Mere Shadow? School Chaplaincy Programs and the Secular State', *University of Queensland Law Journal* 33, no. 1 (2014): 29–41.

286 Patrick, 'Religion, Secularism, and the National School Chaplaincy and Student Welfare Program'.

prevents them from proselytising or making strong truth-claims about their beliefs is problematic. He suggests that an appropriate solution to the issues with the chaplaincy program would be to remove the religious requirement and allow adherents to any faith – or no faith – to perform the role.

In the eyes of these scholars, and based on their own arguments, chaplains perform a role that could be equally well carried out by a non-religious person. While the idea of organisational secularisation provides a means of categorising the tensions involved in a para-church group providing secular employees to government institutions, it does little to address the continuing power of Christianity as a symbol of goodness or worthiness.

Case Study 6: Simultaneous Fights in Queensland

Christian hegemony is declining in Australia. The 2016 Census revealed that, while the number of people who reported having no religion increased in all states, Queensland had the highest proportion of Christians in Australia, with 56% adhering to some form of Christianity. The second-highest percentage of Christians, 55%, was found in New South Wales.[287] It is still possible for Christians to state that they form the majority of Queenslanders. This is, however, a slim majority, composed of adherents to an array of denominations with varying theological and political positions. Nationwide, 30% of Australians report having no religious affiliation – up from 22% at the 2011 Census.[288] Despite these demographic changes, the provisions for religious entry to state schools continue to privilege Christianity and, because chaplaincy is provided alongside religious instruction, offer more formal opportunities for entry than was the case after the 1910 referendum, when 94.6% of Queenslanders adhered to some form of Christianity as did 96% of all Australians.[289]

Outside of chaplaincy, the primary means through which Christianity enters state schools is through religious instruction. Religious instruction is provided for under the *Education (General Provisions) Act* (2006). The section provides for a Minister of Religion or their representative to give students of their denomination religious instruction for up to one hour per week, as appointed by the principal of a state school. In addition, it provides for non-sectarian Bible reading in state primary and special schools. Parents retain the authority to remove their children from any religious instruction or Bible reading,

---

287 Australian Bureau of Statistics, 'Media Release – 2016 Census: Religion', 2016 Census, 27 June 2017, http://www.abs.gov.au/AUSSTATS/abs@.nsf/mediareleasesbyReleaseDate/7E65A144540551D7CA258148000E2B85?OpenDocument.

288 Australian Bureau of Statistics, 'Australia Today – The Way We Live Now', 27 June 2017, http://www.abs.gov.au/ausstats/abs@.nsf/mf/2024.0.

289 Knibbs, 'Census of the Commonwealth of Australia Part 4. Religions', 764–70.

and students in the preparatory year of education are not to receive such instruction.[290]

In legislation, then, the provisions won by the Bible in State Schools League in 1910 remain in effect. Ministers of Religion or approved representatives can enter schools to provide religious instruction. While instruction can legally be provided in the faith of any religious group, when the Queensland government conducted a review of the three most widely used religious instruction curricula, all three were Christian. Further, Bible lessons, so long as they are not sectarian, can be provided. It is unclear how many schools offer these lessons. Parents retain the right to exempt their children from all religious education, including contact with chaplains. This legislative situation, which continues to reflect the results of a referendum that occurred over one hundred years ago, does not go uncontested. Most notably, the QTU opposes religious instruction and school chaplaincy and has stated that the legislation permitting Bible reading should be repealed.[291]

One source of justification for the continued presence of religion in Australian schools has been derived from a cooperative national policy document. The *Melbourne Declaration on Educational Goals for Young Australians* states that a world-class curriculum will enable students "to understand the spiritual, moral, and aesthetic dimensions of life."[292] It also states that schools should produce creative and confident individuals who:

> have a sense of self-worth, self-awareness and personal identity that enables them to manage their emotional, mental, spiritual and physical wellbeing.[293]

This document was agreed to by all Australian Education Ministers. It constitutes a national agreement that is intended to articulate a consistent and positive future for young Australians. It is significant, then, that this declaration includes an explicit reference to 'spiritual' wellbeing. This emphasis indicates that spirituality, not defined as religious faith but potentially interpreted as such, is an important part of a well-rounded education.

---

290   Queensland, Education (General Provisions) Regulations, sec. 76.

291   Queensland Teachers' Union, 'Fact Sheet: Religious Instruction in State Schools', November 2013, http://www.qtu.asn.au/files/1113/8681/3447/Religious_instruction_in_State_Schools_FS_November2013.pdf.

292   Andrew Barr et al., *Melbourne Declaration on Educational Goals for Young Australians*. (ERIC, 2008), 13, https://eric.ed.gov/?id=ED534449.

293   Ibid., 9.

SECULARISATION IN AUSTRALIAN EDUCATION SINCE 1910

This case study explores the discussions surrounding two programs – one religious and one non-religious – which were brought to the centre of public debate in Queensland during the period 2015–2017. In 2016, the Queensland Government reviewed the three most popular collections of materials used for religious instruction in Queensland state schools. This review is examined, alongside the introduction of the Safe Schools Coalition Australia's anti-bullying programme to Queensland state schools, from the second semester of 2015. Safe Schools began in the state of Victoria in 2010, when it was known as the Safe Schools Coalition Victoria. It received federal funding from June 2014 and began a national rollout. The program has been described as "relatively uncontroversial" for "at least the first five years of its existence," with the exception of a "small handful of media articles that were critical of the initiative."[294] In November 2015, shortly after the programme's introduction to Queensland state schools, however, the Safe Schools Coalition Australia introduced *All of Us*, an optional eight-lesson kit which addressed issues such as "homophobia and transphobia; the experiences of intersex people; and the development of alliances between heterosexual, same sex-attracted and transgender students."[295] The review of the religious instruction materials, and the controversy over Safe Schools, occurred more or less simultaneously in Queensland, and commentary occasionally referenced both. While several scholars have examined the discursive construction of Safe Schools in Australian public discourse,[296] no published work to date explores the relationship between the two controversies in this context.

The 2016 review of religious instruction materials was situated within a history of complaints about the content of these materials and the manner in which religious instruction was provided. For instance, in 2010, *The Courier-Mail* reported on calls for religious instruction in state schools to be scrapped, due to students being taught that humans and dinosaurs coexisted.[297] Steve Ryan, then president of the QTU, told the newspaper that some teachers had

---

294 Thompson, 'Predatory Schools and Student Non-Lives', 42.
295 Ibid., 43.
296 Carden, "'Fiddling with Young Kiddies' Minds'"; Thompson, 'Predatory Schools and Student Non-Lives'; Jay Daniel Thompson, 'Your Parents Will Read This: Reading (as) Parents in Journalistic Coverage of the Safe Schools Coalition Australia Controversy', *Journalism* 21, no. 12 (December 2020): 1951–64, https://doi.org/10.1177/1464884918755638; Cover et al., 'Progress in Question'.
297 Carly Hennessey and Kathleen Donaghey, 'Jurasic Class – Schoolkids Taught "Man Walked with Dinosaurs"', *The Courier Mail*, 1 August 2010, 1, Factiva.

TABLE 8 Key moments in the introduction of Safe Schools and the review of religious instruction materials

Date	Event
2010	Safe Schools Coalition Victoria founded
June 2014	Safe Schools Coalition Australia began receiving federal government funding and a national rollout began
July 2015	Safe Schools introduced to Queensland state schools at the start of Semester 2
November 2015	Safe Schools Coalition Australia introduced the optional *All of Us* curriculum
26 February 2016	Federal review into Safe Schools announced
March 2016	Louden report into Safe Schools released
March 2016	Federal government announced changes to Safe Schools program, including a decision not to renew funding
3 June 2016	Matthew Keong, Principal of Windsor State School, announced that he was suspending religious instruction lessons due to problems with the *Connect* curriculum
June 2016	Queensland Minister for Education, Kate Jones, announced a review of the *Connect* materials
18 August 2016	Review of the *Connect* materials released
April 2017	Reviews of *Godspace* and ACCESS ministries materials released
August 2017	Reviews of religious instruction materials revised
October 2017	Funding for Safe Schools in Queensland ran out

to supervise instructors "because of all the fire and brimstone stuff."[298] In the public debate over the religious instruction review, Christian groupings particularly bodies offering religious instruction, and secular groupings, such as Queensland Parents for Secular State Schools, were evident. However, the primary supporters of the religious instruction review, these being teachers and the Queensland Government, do not fit neatly into the category of a "secular" pressure group.

On 3 June 2016, the Principal of Windsor State School, Matthew Keong, wrote to parents announcing that the *Connect* program, then in use at the school, could not be permitted and he was suspending religious instruction lessons. He had only recently discovered that religious instruction programs

---

298 In Carly Hennessey and Kathleen Donaghey, 'Creating a Row at School', *The Courier Mail*, 1 August 2010, 4, Factiva.

SECULARISATION IN AUSTRALIAN EDUCATION SINCE 1910

are not approved or endorsed by the Department of Education. As a result, he undertook his own review of the *Connect* materials and had found that they encouraged instructors to proselytise.[299] Public concern about the Connect materials, centring on a roleplay exercise relating to the story of David and Goliath, had already caused Youthworks to revise the materials.[300]

Before the revision, this roleplay had required children to enact a beheading.[301] Keong's concerns sparked a State Government review of religious instruction programs used in Queensland state schools. The three most widely used programs were reviewed. The first was *Connect*, a program produced by Christian Education Materials and Youthworks Media, and linked to the Sydney Anglican Diocese. The second was the materials produced by ACCESS ministries, an interdenominational Christian group based in Victoria. The third review was of *Godspace*, a program produced by Burst Christian Resources, and associated with the Baptist Churches of New South Wales and the Australian Capital Territory.

The committee reviewing the *Connect* materials indicated that proselytising was unlikely to occur where a child was enrolled in a religious instruction course for the denomination nominated on their enrolment form. In cooperative arrangements, where two denominations work together to provide instruction, proselytising could occur if a child was encouraged to change from one of these faiths to the other. There is no policy relating to whether proselytising occurs when a child who does not identify as Christian is placed by their parents in a Christian religious instruction class.[302] The review found that the majority of the materials were acceptable, with some limited instances requiring removal or amendment.[303] The report suggested that the legislation governing religious instruction should be reconsidered to determine whether the lack of centralised regulation of religious instruction content was in keeping with contemporary community and government expectations.[304]

---

299 Department of Education and Training, 'Report on the Review of the Connect Religious Instruction Materials' (Brisbane: Queensland Government, August 2016), 3, http://educa tion.qld.gov.au/schools/school-operations/docs/report-connect-materials.pdf.

300 Youthworks, 'Response to Connect Articles 21/4/16', *Youthworks Press Releases and Media Announcements* (blog), 21 April 2016, https://www.youthworks.net/press_centre/response -to-connect-articles-21-4-16.

301 Hugh Harris, 'The Horrifying Religious Instruction Classes Planned for Qld Schools', *The Sydney Morning Herald*, 20 April 2016, http://www.smh.com.au/comment/the-horrifying -religious-instruction-classes-planned-for-qld-schools-20160420-gobbpk.html.

302 Department of Education and Training, 'Report on the Review of the Connect Religious Instruction Materials', 6.

303 Ibid.

304 Ibid., i.

While the review of religious instruction materials demonstrated both the government's willingness to examine the programs used by religious groups in state schools and its history of failing to do so, the introduction of Safe Schools highlighted its willingness, however temporary, to support groups that had been traditionally targeted by the Christian Right. The Safe Schools Coalition was a group dedicated to promoting the inclusion of gender and sexually diverse students within Australian schools. It provided materials for schools, including an eight-lesson curriculum, *All of Us*. The program was designed to meet the core outcomes of the Australian Curriculum for Health and Physical Education for students in Years 7 and 8.[305] This was not used by all member schools and, where it is used, it is not always used in its entirety. Membership of the Safe Schools Coalition, and access to the materials, was optional and determined by individual school communities. Safe Schools was introduced to Queensland schools in semester 2 of 2015 to a divided response. The primary public opposition to Safe Schools came from Christian groups, including the ACL. Support, however, was drawn from a broad base, and not predominantly from explicitly secular groups.

A Federal Government review of the Safe Schools Coalition Australia Programme was ordered in 2016. The terms of reference for this review required that the materials provided by the Safe Schools Coalition be examined, and a report provided to advise the extent to which these are consistent with the objections of the programme, suitable for use in schools, age-appropriate, educationally sound, and aligned to the Australian Curriculum. It also sought to determine the extent to which communities were consulted when schools used the resources.[306] The review found that all of the lessons were educationally sound, age-appropriate for early secondary students, and aligned to the curriculum. It also found that, while some activities may not be appropriate in contexts where the families of students had conservative religious views, teachers could make judgements on the use of these activities. Other materials were appropriate for their intended uses. Parental and school board consultation was found to be generally acceptable, but further information and advice on performing this consultation were recommended.[307] The review,

---

305   Chris Bush et al., *All of Us* (Melbourne: Safe Schools Coalition and Minus18, 2015), 8, http://www.education.vic.gov.au/Documents/about/programs/health/AllOfUs_UnitGuide.pdf.

306   Australian Government Department of Education and Training, 'Safe Schools Coalition Australia (SSCA) Programme – Terms of Reference for the Review of the Appropriateness and Efficacy of Programme Resources', 2016, https://docs.education.gov.au/system/files/doc/other/terms_of_reference_-_ssca_-_final.pdf.

307   Bill Louden, *Review of Appropriateness and Efficacy of the Safe Schools Coalition Australia Program Resources* (Department of Education and Training Canberra, 2016), 21–22,

SECULARISATION IN AUSTRALIAN EDUCATION SINCE 1910

conducted by Professor Bill Louden of the University of Western Australia, was broadly positive of the program. This was not evident in the press release sent out by Federal Minister for Education, Simon Birmingham of the conservative Liberal Party. Birmingham's release stated that the review "identified shortcomings that need to be addressed" and referred to "public concern" about the political advocacy of some participant organisations of the Safe Schools Coalition.[308] Despite Louden's support for the materials and his assertion that those activities which were not appropriate for all school situations could be left to teacher discretion, Birmingham outlined the government's plan to:

> Fix the content of the programme resources by:
>
> Having the lesson plans for Lessons 2, 6 and 7 of the All of Us resource amended to remove those activities identified by the review as potentially unsuitable for some students.
>
> Having the content of Lesson 5 of the All of Us resource redesigned to ensure that the content aligns with the curriculum content for biology appropriate for the target age group.
>
> Requiring that the amended resources and any further resources be peer-reviewed and approved by a panel of qualified educators appointed by the Department of Education and Training.[309]

Birmingham also proposed limiting the use of other materials and bolstering the level of parental consent required before lessons and activities associated with Safe Schools could be used. On March 19 2016, changes to the program were officially announced. This included the removal of role-playing scenarios, the removal of material from the Safe Schools Coalition Australia website and transferral to a government website, and a decision not to renew the program's $8 million in funding when it ran out in 2017.[310]

Two petitions – one opposing Safe Schools and one in support – circulated in Queensland in early 2016. The former was circulated by the Queensland chapter of the ACL. It sought a state review of the Safe Schools materials, their suspension while this review occurred, and for the list of schools using the materials to be made public. The latter petition was sponsored by Environment

---

       http://www.parliament.wa.gov.au/publications/tabledpapers.nsf/displaypaper/391409 4c2581904b2f543c2448257fb2000b7d40/$file/tp-4094.pdf.

308   Simon Birmingham, 'Statement on Safe Schools Coalition' | Ministers' Media Centre, Australian Government', 18 March 2016, https://ministers.education.gov.au/birmingham/ statement-safe-schools-coalition.

309   Ibid.

310   Daniel Meers, 'Bullying Program Thumped', *The Courier Mail*, 19 March 2016, 15, Factiva.

Minister Steven Miles. It called for the program to remain in the schools that wanted them and for the list of schools using the program to remain unpublished.[311] The list for Queensland was never made available. The Safe Schools Coalition described negative media responses as highlighting "a high level of confusion" about the type of support provided by Safe Schools and how it operated. It reiterated that all materials were readily accessible online.[312]

Despite the arguments of supporters, the Safe Schools Coalition Australia program ceased on June 30 2017, when federal funding ran out, in New South Wales and South Australia.[313] Before this, it began working with other organisations to ensure that "the legacy of the program's important work lives on."[314] While state funding ended in Queensland in October 2017, schools are still permitted to access materials. In addition to this, the Queensland branch of the Australian Labor Party committed to investing in training and support for teachers, principals, and support staff to work with LGBTI students to prevent bullying and promote equality as part of its 2017 state election policy.[315] At the time of writing, the Labor party remains in power in Queensland, having won re-election again in 2020, suggesting that much of the work done by the Safe Schools Coalition will continue.

It would be simplistic to assume that positions on religious instruction and Safe Schools necessarily align in all cases. Despite this, the temporal proximity of the two cases has encouraged some commentators to speak to both. In particular, there has been a tendency for commentators to deride the State Government for initiating a review into religious instruction but refusing to do the same in response to Safe Schools.

Christian groups were generally opposed to the religious instruction review. One important line of argument was that the review of religious instruction was based on inaccurate assumptions and was unnecessary. For instance, Youthworks, the creators of the *Connect* curriculum, rejected the initial

---

311 Amy Remeikis, 'Stop Safe Schools v Save Safe Schools for Qld Parliament', *Brisbane Times*, 10 March 2016, http://www.brisbanetimes.com.au/queensland/stop-safe-schools-v-save -safe-schools-for-qld-parliament-20160310-gngo72.html.

312 Safe Schools Coalition Australia, 'A Statement from Safe Schools Coalition Australia (SSCA)', *Safe Schools Coalition Australia* (blog), 19 April 2017, http://www.safeschoolscoa lition.org.au/statement-april-2017.

313 Safe Schools Coalition Australia, 'From a Safe Schools Coalition Australia (SSCA) Spokesperson', *Safe Schools Coalition Australia* (blog), 4 May 2017, http://www.safe schoolscoalition.org.au/from-a-safe-schools-coalition-australia-ssca-spokesperson-3.

314 Ibid.

315 The Queensland Branch of the Australian Labor Party, 'Putting Queenslanders First: State Platform 2017' (Australian Labor Party, 2017), 28.

SECULARISATION IN AUSTRALIAN EDUCATION SINCE 1910 89

assertion that *Connect* proselytised. It suggested that work in New South Wales had previously ensured that its materials were appropriate.[316]

A related line of argument was that Matthew Keong, whose concerns about the *Connect* curriculum sparked the review, overstepped his authority in banning the materials from his school. For example, the Uniting Church's newspaper, *Journey*, implied that Keong was personally opposed to religious instruction. It quoted Uniting Church minister Rev Dr Elizabeth Nolan who stated that Keong previously suspended religious instruction in 2014 and 2015 "saying he wanted to review curricula [...] it is a principal's right to review programs being used but not to determine them." It also quoted Queensland Synod moderator Rev David Baker who said "[o]ur concern is that in the Windsor State School example, the policy has not been followed and in removing the program, choice has been removed from parents."[317] These arguments position the religious instruction materials as appropriate and religious organisations as having the right to determine their content.

Christian bodies were also significant in opposing Safe Schools. Two significant lines of argument used by these bodies were that Safe Schools inappropriately taught "gender theory" which was not broadly agreed upon and that the Queensland Government was deceptive in the way it provided the program. One example of the former perspective is found in a document produced by the Australian Catholic Marriage & Family Council, which describes itself as "An Advisory to Australian Catholic Bishops."[318] This document objects to ideas promoted by the Safe Schools Coalition. It singles out the promotion of the picture book, *The Gender Fairy*, which, it says, "includes the message that only the child knows if they are a boy or girl and that no-one else can tell them their gender."[319] The document objects to what it calls "gender theory" and states that:

---

316 Youthworks, 'Response to Education Queensland's Review of "Connect" Curriculum', *Youthworks Press Releases and Media Announcements* (blog), 7 June 2016, https://www .youthworks.net/press_centre/response-to-education-queensland-review-of-connect -curriculum.

317 Mardi Lumsden, 'Christ in the Classroom', *JourneyOnline* (blog), 4 July 2016, https://jour neyonline.com.au/features/christ-in-the-classroom/.

318 Australian Catholic Marriage & Family Council, 'Australian Catholic Marriage & Family Council – An Advisory to Australian Catholic Bishops', accessed 24 July 2017, http://www .acmfc.org.au/.

319 Australian Catholic Marriage & Family Council, 'Information for Parents about Safe Schools Coalition Australia', 3 November 2016, http://www.acmfc.org.au/wp-content/upl oads/2016/11/20160901-Safe-Schools-Coalition-Document-final.pdf.

The Safe Schools Program aims to force children to change the way they understand gender and recognise the differences between boys and girls.[320]

It further describes "gender theory" as "highly contested," and states that "[t]here is a very small number of people who do have real difficulty identifying their biological sex," but that this is a small percentage of the population. It indicates that "[s]exuality is a precious and enormously significant dimension of what it means to be human" and, as such, ought to be within the domain of parental teaching rather than "Government enforced programs."[321]

An example of the second line of argument can be found in the Catholic newspaper *The Catholic Leader*. An article in this newspaper described Safe Schools as a "pernicious program" and asked parents to call for both sides of government to stop the program. It sarcastically noted that:

In Queensland the government is so proud of the program that it won't even disclose which schools have already commenced the program.[322]

Both of these arguments draw on the idea that, in promoting and accepting Safe Schools, the Queensland Government is acting deceptively. Both employ the concept of parental rights, the former by suggesting that parents ought to teach children about sexuality and the latter by requesting that parents call for the program to be stopped. This suggests that education about sexuality is not the proper domain of the school. The tendency of Christian media, in opposing Safe Schools, to appeal to readers as parents has been identified on a national level.[323] These lines of argument mirror some of Joyner's arguments, mentioned in Part 3, about the impropriety of schools teaching content that conflicts with conservative Christian ideologies. They also reflect, to some extent, the arguments of parties who opposed the introduction of religious instruction to state schools by suggesting that religion belongs within the home. The resulting line of argumentation was therefore one in which a clear delineation between "school" and "home" spaces was drawn, with moral and ethical issues positioned as belonging to the "home."

---

320   Ibid., 2.

321   Ibid.

322   David Goodwin, 'UnSafe Schools Destroying Children's Innocence | The Catholic Leader', *The Catholic Leader*, 26 February 2016, http://catholicleader.com.au/analysis/unsaf e-schools-destroying-childrens-innocence.

323   Thompson, 'Your Parents Will Read This'.

SECULARISATION IN AUSTRALIAN EDUCATION SINCE 1910

Opposition to Safe Schools extended well beyond Queensland. This was an issue debated throughout Australia. The ACL has been particularly prominent in these debates, arguing consistently against Safe Schools and indeed referring to the program as "the so-called Safe Schools program."[324] One of the themes running through their opposition to Safe Schools was parental choice: the idea that parents should have the ability to choose whether their children are exposed to ideas about gender and sexuality. Other themes included assertions that Safe Schools did not adhere to new Federal Government requirements after the 2016 review[325] and statements claiming that Safe Schools was not an anti-bullying program but a "radical" program seeking to undermine traditional understandings of sex and gender.[326] The ACL positions itself as a non-denominational group seeking greater influence of Christian ethics on Australian politics, business, and society.[327] In taking a position against Safe Schools, therefore, it seeks to claim a position on behalf of all Christians.

These positions were set against those of the Queensland government and teachers. The then-Minister for Education, Kate Jones, stated that the religious instruction review occurred because:

> The Department of Education has had a long-term policy in place to ensure appropriate material is taught as part of any religious instruction program in state schools
>
> [...]

---

324 Wendy Francis, 'SAFE SCHOOLS – MAKE UP YOUR MIND!', *Australian Christian Lobby* (blog), 26 July 2017, http://www.acl.org.au/safe_schools_make_up_your_mind; Lyle Shelton, 'LGBTIQ Bullying Must Stop', *Australian Christian Lobby* (blog), 10 May 2017, http://www.acl.org.au/lgbtiq_bullying_must_stop; Wendy Francis, 'Finally, Television Is Covering "Safe Schools"', *Australian Christian Lobby* (blog), 17 October 2016, http://www.acl.org.au/finally_television_is_covering_safe_schools; Mark Brown, 'Read the Fine Print: Safe Schools', *Australian Christian Lobby* (blog), 9 May 2017, http://www.acl.org.au/read_the_fine_print_safe_schools.

325 Wendy Francis, 'When Will Children Be Safe from Gender Ideology?', *Australian Christian Lobby* (blog), 9 November 2016, http://www.acl.org.au/when_will_children_by_safe_from_gender_ideology.

326 Wendy Francis, 'Why Parental Concerns with Gender Theory Will Remain', *Australian Christian Lobby* (blog), 23 June 2017, http://www.acl.org.au/why_parental_concerns_with_gender_theory_will_remain.

327 'About The Australian Christian Lobby', Australian Christian Lobby, 2018, https://www.acl.org.au/about.

I am concerned content outside the guidelines of this long-standing policy may currently be being provided in state schools.[328]

This was a clear assertion of the right of the state to determine what is taught in state schools at all times. While the law requires that religious instruction is taught where it is available and that materials are to be provided by the churches or associated bodies, the state retains the right to veto materials that do not meet its strict requirements.

Public pronouncements by the Queensland Government concerning Safe Schools have been limited. However, party documents and statements made to news sources suggest that government and party officials focused on the teacher training aspect of Safe Schools.[329] This, combined with the government's decision not to release the names of schools using the Safe Schools program, suggests an approach that sought to mediate between protecting the rights of LGBTI students and avoiding public controversy to the extent possible.

Making Space and the Limits of Incursion

Cathy Byrne has described Queensland's education system as the least secular system in Australia.[330] For her, a particular concern arose in relation to children who were placed in religious instruction classes with objectionable content, or who witnessed religion enter schools outside of the prescribed times and places. These are real issues. It is also possible to interpret the evidence presented in this part as supporting Byrne's analysis. It would be difficult to support any claim that the backlash against Safe Schools was either disassociated from Christian beliefs or not influential in shaping the decision, first of the Federal Government and then of the State, to defund the program. Similarly, it is undeniable that religious instruction in Queensland prioritises Christianity and that it has continued despite a decline in the proportion of Queenslanders who adhere to that faith. Similarly, the ongoing government funding of chaplaincy has prioritised Christian groups over other faith groups who, while theoretically able to access this funding, rarely do so outside of religious schools.

---

328 Kate Jones, 'Statement from Education Minister Kate Jones', 7 June 2016, http://statements.qld.gov.au/Statement/2016/6/7/statement-from-education-minister-kate-jones.

329 'Kate Jones Denies Safe Schools Cuts in Qld', SBS News, 23 June 2017, https://www.sbs.com.au/news/kate-jones-denies-safe-schools-cuts-in-qld; The Queensland Branch of the Australian Labor Party, 'Putting Queenslanders First: State Platform 2017', 28.

330 Byrne, *Religion in Secular Education*.

SECULARISATION IN AUSTRALIAN EDUCATION SINCE 1910   93

Despite this, the place of Christianity in state schools is limited to selected hours and spaces. For instance, while the legislation does permit the teaching of selected Bible lessons in state schools, this does not appear to be generally promoted or carried out. A suggested reading plan for selected Bible lessons is hosted on the website of the Department of Education and Training.[331] This, however, is not linked to on any page of the Department's website and can only be accessed by using an external search engine. Further, it suggests the use of the *Special Edition of the Good News Bible* which the Religious Education Advisory Committee elected in 2010 to replace with the *Holy Bible – Contemporary English Version, Economy Edition* as the former was out of print.[332] This suggests that this lesson plan is significantly out of date and likely unused. No current plan appears to be available. The current position of Bible reading in Queensland state schools is reminiscent of the fate of the original Bible Readers some of which, as mentioned in Part 2, often remained unopened.

Previous research has explored how the Safe Schools program was positioned and received in public discussions. Cover et al. explored public discussions around the 2016 Safe Schools Coalition review.[333] They uncovered the way three articulations of the grand narrative of progress in these discussions. The first was "that the Safe Schools review disrupts progress of LGBTI community politics,"[334] the second "that the Safe Schools programme is necessary for individual queer developmental progress,"[335] and the third "that the Safe Schools programme is grounded in a politics disruptive to (liberal-humanist and conservative) progress."[336] This last articulation was described by the authors as problematic, relying on the assumption that the LGBTQI movement had been infiltrated by a form of progressive politics that was understood to represent "Marxist-radical-queer." Such a viewpoint, they state, leads Safe

---

331 Religious Education Advisory Committee, 'Selected Bible Lessons Reading Plan for Years 1–7 from Bible Reading in Schools for Use with the Special Edition Good News Bible' (Department of Education and Training, n.d.), https://www.google.com.au/url?sa=t&rct=j&q=&esrc=s&source=web&cd=5&cad=rja&uact=8&ved=0ahUKEwieh5bCxJTVAhXGVLwKHR3nB1kQFgg7MAQ&url=http%3A%2F%2Feducation.qld.gov.au%2Fstudentservices%2Fprotection%2Freligion%2Fdocs%2Fbible_lessons.doc&usg=AFQjCNHQT4IJSga5OVYDTEjNa0t3A77Xig.

332 Religious Education Advisory Committee, 'Minutes: Religious Education Advisory Committee' (Department of Education and Training, 17 November 2010).

333 Cover et al., 'Progress in Question', 6.

334 Ibid., 7.

335 Ibid.

336 Ibid., 9.

Schools to be defined as progressive, meaning radical, but simultaneously seen as an impediment to progress.

Similarly, Shannon and Smith explore media responses to planned school screenings of the documentary *Gayby Baby* and to the *All of Us* teaching kit, part of the Safe Schools program.[337] They use these as case studies to examine the competing imperatives of controversy and diversity. They state that the subject matter of the Safe Schools resources *All of Us* and the OMG (Oh My God) resources, developed by LGBTI-identifying young people to support others dealing with queer issues, were "interpreted by right-wing commentators as patently political in nature."[338] The authors suggest that the controversy over *Gayby Baby* and the Safe Schools materials may have furthered a progressive agenda, leading to increased membership in the Safe Schools Coalition and creative reinterpretation of *Gayby Baby* for use in schools. These developments, they suggest, indicate that it is time to "avoid equating controversy with failure."[339]

The controversy surrounding Safe Schools in Queensland may have contributed to the Queensland Government's decision not to renew the program's funding. The fact that Safe Schools was never banned, despite fervent arguments against its use, suggests that religious fundamentalism does not have the power over school curricula that it once possessed. Many of the same arguments that were levied against MACOS and SEMP were applied to Safe Schools. It was said to be forced on children without parental consent and to change their values. Despite this, the government withstood these conservative pressures. It continued to refuse to release the names of the schools that had joined the Safe Schools Coalition, protecting them from potential harassment.

However, the evidence in this case study also demonstrates the very fragility of degrees of secularisation and desecularisation in contemporary Queensland education. Both the review of religious instruction materials and the introduction of Safe Schools occurred under the purview of the Labor government. This is the less conservative of the two major Australian political parties. Just as the banning of MACOS and SEMP was dependent on the conservative and pietistic worldview of the then-Premier, the events detailed in this part were shaped by the State Government in power at the time.

---

337 Barrie Shannon and Stephen J Smith, 'Dogma before Diversity: The Contradictory Rhetoric of Controversy and Diversity in the Politicisation of Australian Queer-Affirming Learning Materials', *Sex Education* 17, no. 3 (4 May 2017): 242–55, https://doi.org/10.1080/14681811.2017.1302325.

338 Ibid., 248.

339 Ibid., 253.

An additional factor shaping the outcome of this case is the broader societal position of religion. In an environment in which citizens are increasingly disassociated with religion, and those who are religious belong to many faiths, it is more difficult to successfully contest the use of curriculum materials which is perceived to contravene Christian mores. In this environment, the societal separation or differentiation of religion and public institutions may be expected.[340] Despite this increasing disaffiliation of members of the public from traditional religious groups, religion can and does retain significance for many individuals.[341] This is evident in the appeals of the ACL and some members of the public opposing both the review of religious instruction and the introduction of Safe Schools. For these individuals, government control over the school system which is not tempered by Christian influence is seen as threatening.

Conclusion

As this part has demonstrated, the relationship between public schooling in particular and Christianity in Australia is messy, complicated, and contentious. Christian groups continue to assert the right to decide particular content taught in public schools, not only in relation to religious instruction but also in relation to programs that are seen as having a sexuality component. As the second case study in this part demonstrates, the role of individual leaders is significant in determining the outcomes of debates that may arise over the extent to which material taught in schools is in line with religious mores. However, the first case study demonstrates that, while explicitly religious individuals may be hired *for their religiosity* to work in schools as chaplains, their value to school communities must be justified on secular grounds.

Part 5: Conclusion

The definition of secularisation applied in this book does not presume that there is a necessary or linear relationship between modernisation and secularisation. It allows for an understanding of the complicated relationship between religious and secular impulses in education whereby, despite the presumption of the existence of a secular education system, religious groups can make claims to determine the content and nature of education.

---

340   Dobbelaere, *Secularization*; Tschannen, 'The Secularization Paradigm: A Systematization'.
341   E.g. Possamai, *Religion and Popular Culture*, 32.

The shifting nature of secularisation is evident not only in the outcomes of the conflicts explored in this book but also in the terminology used to justify positions on either side. The problem of a binary opposition between religion and secular ideals was highlighted in Part 2. As I have previously noted, the terms religion and secular elude any attempts to construct a universal definition, with the definition of 'religion' in particular remaining a site of contestation.[342] These definitional issues are exacerbated by the problem of the purported binary opposition between religious and secular ideals. As Chavura has shown, the reality of the secular ideal in Australian history cannot be understood if 'secular' and 'religious' are presumed to be binary opposites.[343]

The case studies in this work support Chavura's argument. The terms 'secular' and 'Christian' have undergone considerable change during the studied period. In particular, their relationship with one another has shifted. This is most evident in the first case study. The Bible in State Schools League sought to replace the 'secular' education system of Queensland with the 'secular' system of New South Wales. The outcome of the referendum led to the word 'secular' being removed from the Queensland legislation. However, during the period of conflict, two competing definitions of this word operated within Queensland political discourse.

Through exploring schooling as an institution, I have resisted the desire to examine secularisation at a whole-of-society level. Recognising the multi-scalar and multi-faceted nature of secularisation helps to overcome a tendency to differentiate merely between religion in the public and the private sphere, with the 'private' sphere understood as an effectively sacred space that is outside of the scope of analysis.[344] This approach also allows for a recognition of the reality that religious entrepreneurs can fill 'archipelagos' in which everyday life can be resacralised.[345] This is evident in the second case study, where clusters of German Lutheran churches in South-East Queensland sought to retain a balance between engagement with the secular system of state education and the

---

342 E.g. Steve Bruce, 'Defining Religion: A Practical Response', *International Review of Sociology* 21, no. 1 (March 2011): 107–20, https://doi.org/10.1080/03906701.2011.544190; Victoria S Harrison, 'The Pragmatics of Defining Religion in a Multi-Cultural World', *International Journal for Philosophy of Religion* 59, no. 3 (June 2006): 133–52, https://doi.org/10.1007/s11153-006-6961-z; James McLachlan, 'Kevin Schilbrack on Defining Religion and the Field of the Study of Religions', *Sophia* 53, no. 3 (1 September 2014): 379–82, https://doi.org/10.1007/s11841-014-0445-x; Hans Schilderman, ed., *The Concept of Religion: Defining and Measuring Contemporary Beliefs and Practices* (Leiden; Boston: Brill, 2014).

343 Chavura, "'… but in Its Proper Place….'" Religion, Enlightenment, and Australia's Secular Heritage'.

344 Dobbelaere, *Secularization*, 103.

345 Wilford, 'Sacred Archipelagos', 343.

continuation of their religious and cultural practices through the operation of German schools. These German Lutheran communities were separated from the society around them through language, background, and, during World War One, by wartime suspicions. It is also evident the religiously-motivated banning of MACOS and SEMP, whereby Queensland itself became in a sense a sacred archipelago due to the force of its Premier's religious beliefs. Viewed alongside the justifications given for the introduction of Federal Government funding for non-government schools. the banning of MACOS and SEMP demonstrates that arguments appealing to Christian beliefs had greater currency in Queensland than they did in Australia as a whole.

One of the key ways in which the multi-faceted nature of secularisation was examined in this work was through the exploration of cases at multiple scales. These cases have demonstrated the potential for the relationship between Christian and secular ideals to be very different on a local than a state level, and different again on a national level. This also suggests the relevance of multiple modernities to analyses of secularisation. Eisenstadt's concept of "multiple modernities" highlights the fact that modernisation is not a clear process that is identical throughout the world.[346] Likewise, secularisation is not an even or predictable process. While the historical and contemporary scholarship on the relationship between Christian and 'secular' impulses in Australian education suggests the ongoing experiences of incursion, proselytising, and the privileging of Christian over other belief systems, the theory of secularisation can reveal the extent to which such experiences are contextually and historically contingent.

Acknowledgements

This work began life as my doctoral dissertation. My sincere gratitude is due, as always, to my incomparable supervisors, the "dream team" of Dr Margaret Gibson and Professor Barbara Pini.

Thanks are also due to Professor Stephen G. Parker for his incredible patience with me as I completed this work during the strange period that has been 2020–2021.

---

346 Eisenstadt, 'Multiple Modernities'.

Printed in the United States
by Baker & Taylor Publisher Services